Latino Voices

Latino Voices

Mexican, Puerto Rican, and Cuban Perspectives on American Politics

Rodolfo O. de la Garza,
Louis DeSipio, F. Chris Garcia,
John Garcia, and Angelo Falcon

Westview Press

BOULDER • SAN FRANCISCO • OXFORD

To William A. Diaz
Friend and Colleague

This Westview softcover edition is printed on acid-free paper and bound in library-quality, coated covers that carry the highest rating of the National Association of State Textbook Administrators, in consultation with the Association of American Publishers and the Book Manufacturers' Institute.

Published in 1992 in the United States of America by Westview Press, Inc., 5500 Central Avenue, Boulder, Colorado 80301-2877, and in the United Kingdom by Westview Press, 36 Lonsdale Road, Summertown, Oxford OX2 7EW

A CIP catalog record for this book is available from the Library of Congress.
ISBN 0-8133-8724-8

Printed and bound in the United States of America

 The paper used in this publication meets the requirements of the American National Standard for Permanence of Paper for Printed Library Materials Z39.48-1984.

10   9   8   7   6   5   4   3   2

Contents

1

The Latino National Political Survey

Pundits and politicians have in recent decades become increasingly concerned about the nation's "Spanish-origin" populations. Among the questions they ask are How much do Latinos[1] support fundamental American values? How willing are they to learn English? Are Hispanics liberal or conservative, Republicans or Democrats? Is it better or more accurate to refer to them as Hispanics or as Latinos?

The need to answer questions such as these gave rise to the Latino National Political Survey (LNPS). Future volumes will thoroughly analyze its results. In this volume, our objective is much more modest: to provide basic information about the political values, attitudes and behaviors of the Mexican-, Puerto Rican-, and Cuban-origin populations in the United States.

There are several reasons why politicians, the press, and the American public are now interested in Hispanic populations. One is demographic. From 1970 to 1980, Hispanics went from 9.1 to 14.6 million, an increase of 60 percent. By 1990, they increased by another 47 percent, to 21.4 million. A second is that this growth has been accompanied by geographic dispersion and changes in the national origins of the group. Historically, the great majority of this population was of Mexican origin and concentrated in the Southwest, including California. Today, this population is visible in virtually every major city in the country and includes large concentrations of Cubans and Puerto Ricans as well as identifiable clusters of groups from the Caribbean (Haitians and Dominicans), from Central America (Salvadorans, Guatemalans, and Nicaraguans), and growing concentrations of Latin American nationalities.

A third factor is increased political clout. For several reasons, including mushrooming activism and the expanded protections of the Voting Rights Act, the number of "Spanish-origin" representatives has increased rapidly. In Arizona, California, Florida, New Mexico, New York, and Texas, this expansion outpaced population growth between 1973 and 1990 (Pachon and DeSipio 1992). This growth rate reflects both recent dramatic gains and the historical exclusion of this population from elective office.

The nation's knowledge about this group has lagged behind its interest in it, and this knowledge gap has become fertile ground for claims and counterclaims about Hispanics—who they are and what their presence portends for the nation. Non-Latinos rooted in or nurtured by historically grounded anti-Hispanic biases expressed alarm. Their fears, fueled by unsubstantiated claims, contributed to creating the climate that produced the Official English movement and the anti-Hispanic dimensions of the Immigration Reform and Control Act of 1986 (de la Garza and Trujillo 1991; de la Garza 1992). Although neither of these focuses exclusively on Latinos, there is no question that both target Hispanics.

Indicative of that national mood is a 1990 national poll that found that, compared to Jews, blacks, Asians, and southern whites, Americans perceive Latinos as second only to blacks in terms of being lazy rather than hard-working and as living off welfare rather than being self-supporting (Smith 1990). The survey also reports that Hispanics are seen as the nation's least-patriotic group. Nationally influential individuals such as Senator Alan Simpson (R-WY), former governor Richard Lamm (D-CO), and Michael Teitelbaum of the Arthur P. Sloan Foundation share this latter concern and have gone so far as to suggest that Latinos threaten the physical and political integrity of the nation (Fuchs 1990: 255-256).

Unlike Anglos, Latinos reacted positively to demographic increases, and many made equally unsubstantiated claims about how this growth would affect the nation. Perhaps the most vivid illustration of hopeful and exaggerated projections was that the 1980s would be the "Decade of the Hispanic." The assertion was that with increased numbers, Latino political clout would influence the outcome of the presidential election of 1980; when that did not materialize, they made a stronger claim for the 1984 election, and then the 1988 election (de la Garza and DeSipio 1992). Similarly, they predicted that their new political clout would make itself felt in legislation emanating from Congress and statehouses across the nation. Without doubt, Latino influence did increase in these legislatures; equally true is that this influence did not approximate what had been predicted.

Similar unsubstantiated claims were made regarding other aspects of Hispanic life. Market analysts proclaimed the existence of a distinct "Hispanic market" unified by language and other cultural styles (Caplan 1987). More significantly, leaders in the commercial world and in politics spoke and acted as if the Spanish-origin populations constituted a community, that is, a relatively homogeneous population with a common culture and shared political and economic interests. Whether this group was identified as Hispanics or Latinos was less significant than the assertion that a coherent group existed and must be recognized.

Politically, the group came to be recognized. By 1984, the potential of the Latino vote was such that both parties claimed to have won the support of the Latino community. Democrats pointed to the historical support they had received from Mexican Americans and to the continued support they received in the barrios of the Southwest to document that they continued to win the great majority of Latino votes. Republicans emphasized that they had made major inroads into the Hispanic community because Republicans appealed to traditional Hispanic values such as religion, the family, and the work ethic. Scholars and columnists who analyzed the results of the 1984 campaign concluded, however, that neither assertion could be believed because neither was supported by reliable data (de la Garza 1987).

The principal reason for questioning these and other claims regarding Latinos is that neither in 1984 nor since have independent national surveys and public opinion polls systematically included Latinos as a separate population whose social and political attitudes and behaviors could be analyzed. Moreover, when Latinos are included, the several subgroups are not identified separately so as to know whether the views presented are those of Mexican-, Puerto Rican-, or Cuban-origin respondents. As is shown throughout this volume, on many important issues there are key differences among these groups, and therefore it is necessary to identify whose views are being cited.

Thus, until now, there have been no reliable national data indicating whether Latinos support "traditional" values, as Republicans claim. Moreover, Republicans claim generalized Hispanic support when what they have received is overwhelming support from Cubans in Florida. At the state and local levels within Florida, furthermore, Cuban Republicanism is somewhat tenuous (Grenier 1991). Also, there are reasons to suspect that Republican polls describing Latino support oversample the small number of affluent Latinos who live in mixed or majority Anglo neighborhoods, that is, those who are most likely to vote Republican. In short, Republican claims about Latino support are not believable.

Democratic claims are also suspect. Their reports seem to ignore the decline in Democratic affiliation and voting among younger voters and among the better-educated and more affluent (F. C. Garcia 1987). Also, many of the data on Mexican Americans have been produced from surveys that oversample low-income areas in Southern California and South Texas, that is, barrios that are the core of traditional Democratic partisanship in two major states. To the extent that Democrats rely on such data for generalizing about Latinos, they overstate Mexican American (and Puerto Rican) support for their party.

These partisan exaggerations reflect a fundamental problem for Hispanics. The nation's politics continues to be conducted without the systematic inclusion of Latino voices. This is because national public opinion polls, including those supported by public funds such as the National Election Study, have not made the same effort to include Latinos that they have made to include African Americans. Consequently, it is impossible to document Latino concerns in the same way that the concerns of other Americans, including African Americans, are documented. To the extent that the results of such surveys play a role in determining candidates and influencing policy, this means that Latinos are effectively denied the opportunity to influence these processes.

Furthermore, because we do not know what Latinos themselves think, others, including well-intentioned Latino leaders and anti-Hispanic Anglos, are free to claim that they represent Latinos or accurately describe Latino views. This gives rise to debates about what the "people" really think and who speaks for them. For example, Linda Chavez, to whom television news programs often turn when they want the Hispanic perspective, indicts Latino leaders for inaccurately representing Hispanic views of bilingual education and the extent to which Hispanics speak English and support learning English (Chavez 1991). Somewhat to our surprise, our findings completely contradict her arguments (see Tables 7.19 - 7.21).

A. Design and Implementation
of the Latino National Political Survey

It was to provide reliable information regarding such fundamental issues that the LNPS was designed and implemented. Thus, the first objective of the LNPS was to collect basic data describing Latino political values, attitudes, and behavior. This includes information on (1) support for core American values, including several types of ideological indicators; (2) attitudes toward other groups, including Hispanics and Anglos, that are relevant to coalition building; (3) attitudes toward major social issues such as abortion, affirmative action, and women's rights that address long-standing assumptions about Latino cultures; (4) foreign policy perspectives that are relevant to questions about patriotism and irredentism; (5) partisanship and voting practices that respond to competing claims; and (6) political behaviors such as organizational memberships, problem-solving strategies, participation in ethnically related activities, and involvement with schools that will indicate how and to what extent Latinos engage the polity in efforts to improve their lives.

In addition to gathering this baseline political information, the LNPS also collected demographic information on the respondents (see chapters

2 and 3). Those familiar with survey research will note that these demographics are extraordinarily detailed regarding ethnic indicators. This is to help us measure as precisely as possible the characteristics that distinguish Hispanics. For example, commercial and political surveys seldom indicate if respondents are native- or foreign-born, and they usually ignore language capabilities. The LNPS traces familial histories for three generations and measures language competence subjectively and objectively. Also, virtually all surveys equate national origin with ethnic identity; that is, they assume Latinos of varying national origins identify as Latinos, rather than with their national origin. The LNPS separates national origin from ethnicity. It determines an individual's national heritage, and with a series of questions it then determines the extent to which that person identifies ethnically. LNPS respondents of Mexican origin, for example, may identify as Mexicanos, Hispanos, Americans, or with some combination of these or other identities. Similarly, surveys that include Hispanics, blacks, and whites often report differences between blacks and whites and note that "Hispanics may be of any racial group." The LNPS asks its respondents how they identify racially and includes that response as a separate ethnic indicator.

The LNPS, thus, was designed to combine detailed demographic data with extensive attitudinal and behavioral data to answer the following key questions:

1. What are the fundamental political values of Latinos in the United States?
2. What principal factors have influenced these values?
3. How stable are these values across age cohorts, national-origin groups, and regions?
4. What patterns characterize Hispanic political attitudes and behavior?
5. How stable are these attitudes and behaviors across age cohorts, national-origin groups, and regions?
6. How are political values related to the political attitudes and behavior of Latinos?
7. What effect do gender, immigration history, citizenship status, socioeconomic status, and community characteristics have on Hispanic political values, attitudes, and behaviors?
8. Is there a distinct Latino, as opposed to Mexican American, Puerto Rican, or Cuban, political community in the United States? If not, is there a basis from which such a political community may emerge?
9. What are the significant differences and similarities regarding political values, attitudes, and behaviors among Hispanic subgroups and between Latinos and non-Latinos?

Our efforts to analyze the data and answer these questions are ongoing. As of June 1992, eight papers have been presented at academic conferences. These have focused on self-labeling (J. Garcia et al. 1991), ideology (F. C. Garcia et al. 1991), support for core American values (de la Garza et al. forthcoming; de la Garza et al. 1992a; de la Garza et al. 1992b), partisanship (F. C. Garcia et al. 1992), political participation (Falcon et al. 1991) and foreign policy perspectives (de la Garza et al. 1992c). We expect to combine that work into two comprehensive volumes. At that time, we plan to make the survey results available as a public-use file.

B. Speaking for Themselves

In this volume, we present data in the format most often used by public officials and the press; that is, we describe the extent to which U.S. citizens of Hispanic origins hold particular views and participate in specific activities. Additionally, because noncitizens constitute 37.7 percent of the Latino adult population, compared to 3.1 percent of non-Hispanics, we also present selected data on noncitizens (U.S. Bureau of the Census, Current Population Reports 1991a: Table One [hereafter Census]).

We think it is important to keep the attitudes and behaviors of citizens and noncitizens separate. Failure to do so distorts any description of the relationship Latinos have to the polity. For example, more than half of all Hispanics who did not vote in 1990 were ineligible to vote because they were not U.S. citizens (NALEO 1991: vi). Thus, calculating voter participation without distinguishing citizens from noncitizens seriously understates Latino voting. For example, in the 1988 presidential election, 28.8 percent of all Latino adults voted. Among Latino U.S. citizen adults, fully 45.9 percent voted (NALEO 1992: 6). Additionally, noncitizen views are seldom heard. Since this is a population that may soon join the polity, it is in the interests of Latinos and the nation to be informed about its views (NALEO 1989).

We think that presenting our data in this format will maximize their relevance to contemporary political debates. They illustrate the views of different groups and indicate the issues on which the groups differ as well as those on which there is agreement. For example, given the acrimonious debate over bilingual education, it is important to know that over 80 percent of Mexican, Puerto Rican, and Cuban U.S. citizens support bilingual education. Latinos, in other words, are essentially of one voice on this issue. Furthermore, even greater percentages of each group indicate that the objectives of bilingual education are to have students learn English exclusively or to have them learn English and Spanish.

Contrary to the claims of supporters of the Official English movement, Latinos see bilingual education as a way to learn English and they strongly support access to this opportunity.

This volume, then, presents information that should inform our discussion about Latino politics. It tells us how Hispanics view and act on the political world; it does not tell us why they think as they do, nor does it suggest how to change their views and behaviors. Those are questions that our research will address in the future.

C. Methodology

The Hispanics included in this study are Mexicans, Puerto Ricans, and Cubans eighteen years of age or older. There are several reasons for this. First is that we share the view that recognizes the several Latino national-origin populations as distinctive (Bean and Tienda 1987: 2) and consider it culturally demeaning and conceptually indefensible to aggregate a priori all these groups under a single label such as Hispanic or Latino. Thus, we could not survey "Hispanics" without targeting specific populations. Given the nation's large number of distinct Latino national-origin groups, however, it would have been technically and financially impossible to survey representative samples of each. Therefore, the LNPS included Mexicans, Cubans, and Puerto Ricans because they are the largest and politically the most significant Latino national-origin groups. As of March 1990, the Census Bureau estimated that Mexicans constituted approximately 64 percent of all Hispanics, while Puerto Ricans and Cubans were 11 and 5 percent, respectively (Census 1991b). Together, they account for almost 80 percent of the nation's Hispanics and an even greater proportion of the nation's Latino U.S. citizens.

In total, the LNPS includes 1,546 Mexicans, 589 Puerto Ricans, and 682 Cubans. For our purposes, a respondent was defined as a member of one of these groups if he or she, one parent, or two grandparents were solely of Mexican, Puerto Rican, or Cuban ancestry. Those members of these groups not represented in the survey are those living in states whose combined Mexican, Puerto Rican, and Cuban populations are less than 5 percent Latino and those living in communities within selected states that have a combined total of less than 3 percent Mexican, Puerto Rican, and Cuban residents. The survey was conducted in 40 Standard Metropolitan Statistical Areas (see Table 1.1). The sample is representative of 91 percent of the Mexican, Puerto Rican, and Cuban populations in the United States.

The survey also included 456 non-Hispanic whites (Anglos). The Anglo sample is representative of Anglos residing in the areas listed;

TABLE 1.1 Survey Sites for the Latino National Political Survey

Boston, MA	New York, NY	Nassau-Suffolk, NJ
Newark, NJ	Jersey City, NJ	Chicago, IL
Philadelphia, PA	Miami, FL	Tampa-St. Petersburg, FL
Houston, TX	San Antonio, TX	Dallas-Ft. Worth, TX
El Paso, TX	Lamb County, TX	Corpus Christi, TX
Albuquerque, NM	Phoenix, AZ	Denver-Boulder, CO
Riverside, CA	San Diego, CA	Los Angeles-Long Beach, CA
Fresno, CA	San Jose, CA	Hartford, CT
Austin, TX	Sacramento, CA	Kansas City, MO/KS
Bakersfield, CA	Las Vegas, NV	Portland-Vancouver, OR/WA
Anaheim-Santa Ana-	Gary-Hammond-	New Brunswick-Perth
Garden Grove, CA	East Chicago, IN	Amboy- Sayreville, NJ
Fort Lauderdale-	Paterson-Clinton	Brownsville-Harlingen-
Hollywood, FL	Passaic, NJ	San Benito, TX
Eddy County, NM	San Francisco-	McAllen-Edinberg-
Santa Cruz, CA	Oakland, CA	Mission, TX

however, since these sites were selected to represent Latinos rather than the nation, the Anglos included here are not necessarily representative of Anglos nationwide.

The survey began in August 1989 and ended in April 1990. Over 97 percent of the interviews were completed by February 1990. These were in-person interviews, and respondents had the choice of being interviewed in Spanish or English; 60 percent selected Spanish. Additional methodological information may be found in Appendix 2.

We made great efforts to ensure that the LNPS was well designed and implemented. With support from the Ford Foundation, a research team consisting of Rodolfo O. de la Garza, Angelo Falcon, F. Chris Garcia, and John A. Garcia began a feasibility study in 1987. The feasibility study completed, we received support from the Ford Foundation, the Rockefeller Foundation, the Spencer Foundation, and the Tinker Foundation to complete the LNPS. This included a major bibliographic project (F. C. Garcia et al. 1991) and extensive research into issues such as sample design, whether the survey should utilize in-person or telephone surveys, the significance of dialectical differences among Spanish speakers, and the extent to which the survey should focus on new issues or replicate prior research (F.C. Garcia et al. 1989).

We were greatly assisted in our deliberations by distinguished colleagues from across the country. Steve Heringa of the University of Michigan's Institute for Social Research advised us regarding sample design issues. We invited the leading survey research centers in the nation to submit proposals for conducting the research, and he helped us evaluate these. After careful scrutiny, we selected Temple University's Institute for Survey Research to conduct the survey. Robert Santos, the sampling statistician for the 1979 National Chicano Survey, served as Temple's project director. After our survey was completed, the National Science Foundation evaluated the LNPS sample and approved it for incorporation into the ongoing Panel Study of Income Dynamics. We are therefore completely confident in the quality of the sample.

We emphasize this because many of the results that we have made public challenge what many of us have long assumed were unassailable truths. The first response of critics who would sustain those shibboleths has been to challenge the sample's representativeness. Rather than focus on the sample, therefore, we would encourage those who are discomfited by these results to focus on other dimensions of the study, including how to conceptualize and operationalize the questions that interest them. They might also find it useful to reexamine their assumptions, as we have begun to do.

The broad outline of what we hoped to accomplish included much more than we could realize. The LNPS National Advisory Board, consisting of Amado Padilla, Alejandro Portes, Steve Rosenstone, Carole Uhlaner, and Linda Williams, provided keen advice that helped us sharpen our focus. Carole Uhlaner was especially generous with her time and insights.

The items included in the questionnaire derive from several sources. To enable us to provide baseline data for Latinos regarding issues on which the attitudes of the general public are well documented, we took questions directly from established surveys, such as the National Election Study, the General Social Survey, the National Chicano Survey, and the Times Mirror Study of the American Electorate. We drew on our own work to create many new items, and we borrowed items directly from the work of Robert Bach, Bruce Cain, Harry Pachon, Amado Padilla, Alejandro Portes, Carole Uhlaner, and Sidney Verba. Having benefited from their advice and experiences, the decisions regarding the survey questions were made by Rodolfo O. de la Garza, Angelo Falcon, F. Chris Garcia, and John A. Garcia.

The feasibility study that preceded the LNPS also contributed to generating questions. The bibliographic research informed us about what areas were in greatest need of research. A series of focus group interviews that we conducted as part of the feasibility study helped us identify issues and create questions that otherwise might have been overlooked.

D. Reading the Tables

The chapters that follow share a common format. Each begins with a synopsis describing what we consider to be the most important findings of the series of related tables that are then presented. With each set of synopses, we provide a list of the survey questions used to produce that set of tables. The exact wording of each question is contained in Appendix 1.

The tables also follow a common format. All of them are based on weighted data (see Appendix 2). The first number in each column indicates how many of each national-origin group selected each of the possible responses to the question that was asked; the second figure indicates the percentage of that group that gave this answer. The sum at the bottom of each column indicates how many from each national-origin group answered the question. Thus, in Table 1.2, 586 Mexicans, or 38.3 percent of all Mexican respondents, strongly support bilingual education. A total of 1,529 respondents of Mexican origin responded to this question.

In some cases, we combine a series of interrelated questions into a single table and report the number of respondents who gave a particular response. For example, Table 8.11 indicates how many respondents reported that they had participated in each of the specified activities. In this type of table, we list the number of respondents who answered each

TABLE 1.2   Attitude Toward Bilingual Education, by National Origin

Attitude Toward Bilingual Education	Mexican	Puerto Rican	Cuban
Strongly support	586	233	256
	38.3%	39.7%	38.0%
Support	711	279	356
	46.5%	47.5%	52.8%
Uncertain	160	42	39
	10.5%	7.2%	5.8%
Oppose	52	23	12
	3.4%	3.9%	1.8%
Strongly oppose	20	10	11
	1.3%	1.7%	1.6%
Total	1,529	587	674
	100.0%	100.0%	100.0%

Note: Throughout the volume, percentages are rounded.

of the questions that make up each cell and do not list a total for the respective national-origin columns.

The tables present weighted data. The use of weighted data ensures that the sample is representative of the Mexican, Puerto Rican, and Cuban populations of the United States. The percentages presented in each cell present the true weighted proportion of respondents in the national population answering the particular question in the manner indicated. For the sake of clarity, we present rounded whole numbers to indicate the respondents in each cell. Thus, the 586 Mexican respondents who strongly support bilingual education in Table 1.2 represent anywhere from 585.5 to 586.49 weighted answers. The calculation of percentages based on the weighted values explains the seemingly anomalous situations of cell values of zero having a nonzero percentage (an example of this situation appears in Table 2.3) or of the whole number values in the cells not summing to the column total (see Table 2.1).

We refer to the respondent's national-origin group as "RG" (respondent's group). In several questions, we asked respondents about other members of their national-origin group. In these cases, instead of formulating different questions for each national-origin group, we used one question and asked members of each group to answer it with reference to their own RG.

As we indicated previously, Anglos in this sample may not be representative of all white non-Hispanics. Also, the Anglos reported on in this volume are not the entire "non-Latino" sample from the survey. We excluded 145 non-Latino respondents, including African Americans, Hispanics who trace their ancestry to parts of Latin America other than Mexico, Cuba, and Puerto Rico, and immigrants not of European origin. Appendix 1 indicates which questions were asked of Anglos.

We did not ask all questions of all respondents, and not all respondents answered all the questions asked them. For this reason, the total number of respondents varies from question to question. In general, we did not ask questions that were inappropriate, given the respondent's circumstances. For example, we did not ask non-U.S. citizens about electoral participation in U.S. elections, from which they are statutorily excluded, and we did not ask Anglos questions about Latino ethnicity. Also, because of time considerations and the availability of comparable data elsewhere, we did not ask the Anglos we interviewed many of the questions that we borrowed from other surveys. Also, because of the issues involved, we sometimes present our data in terms of the respondent's gender and educational characteristics. In every case, however, each of the Latino national-origin groups responded to each question.

Although it is not possible to itemize the respondent pool for each question, we can provide the maximum number of respondents in each of the categories around which the volume's chapters are organized.

Chapter 2 distinguishes between the foreign- and the native-born. The total number of possible respondents for each group is 781 foreign-born and 765 native-born Mexicans; 387 and 202 foreign- and native-born Puerto Ricans, respectively; and 587 foreign-born and 92 native-born Cubans. There are only 21 foreign-born Anglos compared with 435 native-born. These characteristics are essential to understanding Hispanic political incorporation. In the case of Mexicans and Cubans, to be foreign-born implies being a noncitizen from a Latin American environment. Puerto Ricans born in Puerto Rico are from a similar cultural environment, but they are U.S. citizens by birth. Thus, while Puerto Ricans are not literally "foreign-born," they share some fundamental characteristics with Mexican and Cuban immigrants. Therefore, in chapter 2, we classify Puerto Ricans born in Puerto Rico as foreign-born. Chapters 3 through 9 include all but two Puerto Ricans[2], whether they were born in Puerto Rico or the continental United States, and all Mexicans, Cubans, and Anglos who are native-born or naturalized U.S. citizens. Chapters 3 through 9 include 878 Mexicans (472 female and 406 male), 587 Puerto Ricans (327 female and 260 male), 312 Cubans (172 female and 140 male), and 446 Anglos (216 female and 230 male). In chapter 10, we examine characteristics of non-U.S. citizens. Although two of the Puerto Rican respondents and ten of the Anglo respondents are not citizens, their small number necessitates that we exclude them from the analysis. Instead, the tables focus on the 668 Mexicans (267 female and 401 male) and 367 Cubans (193 female and 174 male) who are not U.S. citizens.

Before examining the tables, we would like to suggest one note of caution. Although the survey presents data on the three largest Latino national-origin populations, it does not presume to present a picture of what all Latinos think or do. First, it cannot speak to the 21 percent of Latino national-origin groups who were not surveyed. Second, the three surveyed national-origin groups do not make up equal shares of the Latino population. To reflect "Hispanic" views accurately, that is to present an integrated perspective for all the groups, therefore, it is essential to have the concerns of several of the national-origin groups proportionally represented in whatever is discussed. For reasons that are not easily explained, however, the information that the press makes available to the nation does not reflect the relative proportion of these groups. An analysis of newspapers in each of the cities included in the LNPS while the survey was being conducted found that among references to specific national-origin groups as opposed to the more generic Latino or Hispanic, Cuban Americans are by far the most likely . . . to be mentioned . . . .

Latino-content stories originating in Florida are more likely to be carried by papers outside of Florida than are stories originating in any of the other states under study . . . .

Latino stories carried nationwide, though rare, more often than not involve Cuban Americans or events taking place in Miami. No uniquely Mexican American or Puerto Rican event can make a similar claim to the generation of national news. (DeSipio and Henson 1992: 11)

Consequently, given the differences between Cubans and other groups and given that Cubans are a small percentage of all Latinos, this information may have misinformed the nation about the Hispanic population. Nevertheless, if Mexicans, Puerto Ricans, and Cubans have similar beliefs or positions on an issue, it is safe to say that there is a "Latino" perspective. As presented here, however, it is not possible to average the positions of these three national-origin groups and present the result as the "Latino position." The survey was carefully designed to describe the views and activities of each group. We hope that the reader will use the information with the same caution.

E. Findings

What, then, does the LNPS tell us? Particularly among citizens, it illustrates that Mexicans, Puerto Ricans, and Cubans have a great deal in common, but they also differ in significant ways on important issues. Thus, there may be a Hispanic political community, but its parameters do not fit any existing presuppositions.

Our respondents do not primarily identify as members of a Hispanic or Latino community. Instead, the three groups overwhelmingly prefer to identify in national-origin terms such as Mexican American, Puerto Rican, or Cuban. A surprisingly small percentage of each group prefers to identify in pan-ethnic terms such as Latino or Hispanic. It is particularly noteworthy that more respondents prefer to be called "American" than "Latino," the label that many members of the Latino intelligentsia, including ourselves, have insisted is both the "correct" and the preferred label. Equally significant, only a small proportion of these groups prefer to identify as "Hispanics," the term most used by government, media, and advertisers.

Relatedly, to the extent that the Hispanic political community exists, there is scant evidence that it is rooted in alleged distinctive cultural traditions such as Spanish-language maintenance, religiosity, or shared identity. Mexicans, Puerto Ricans, and Cubans have little interaction with each other, most do not recognize that they have much in common culturally, and they do not profess strong affection for each other. Furthermore, especially among Mexicans, the native-born do not evidence strong Spanish maintenance. Additionally, they are not particularly likely to indicate that religion significantly influences their daily lives.

Nonetheless, these groups do have much in common regarding their views of many domestic policy issues. They favor increased government spending on health and crime and drug control; education; the environment; child services; and bilingual education. They also overwhelmingly look to government to solve the problems that most concern them. Thus, large majorities of each group support what may reasonably be called core elements of a liberal domestic agenda. Furthermore, on those issues where it is possible to make comparisons with Anglos, the Latino groups are notably more liberal. These responses are what we would have expected from Mexicans and Puerto Ricans; it is surprising that Cubans also hold these views. Clearly, a unified Hispanic agenda could be developed around these issues.

Expanding this agenda beyond these issues would be problematic, however, because the groups differ regarding their attitudes toward most other domestic issues. More significantly, a group may hold liberal positions on some issues, and on others it has conservative views. For example, Puerto Ricans support increased spending on welfare and programs intended to help blacks, but they take a conservative position on abortion and, along with Mexicans and Cubans, support capital punishment. Cubans strongly reject affirmative action and do not support increased spending on welfare and black-oriented programs, but hold liberal views on abortion.

Group-based differences in partisanship indicate that it is inappropriate to discuss "Hispanic" partisanship as if it were a pattern that characterized all groups. Instead, as expected, most Mexicans and Puerto Ricans are Democrats, and most Cubans are Republicans. Mexicans and Puerto Ricans report a lower level of Democratic partisanship than might have been expected, however, and a substantial number of Mexican Republicans are former Democrats. On the other hand, although the majority are Republican, more Cubans are either Democrats or lean in that direction and fewer strongly identify as Republicans than we might have predicted.

Surprisingly, perhaps, a majority of each group identifies as moderate to conservative ideologically. This orientation may be reflected in how positively each group views American society. Substantial majorities indicate they have never experienced discrimination. Similarly, the great majority of those who had contacts with government indicated they were treated fairly and that they were satisfied with the results of their contacts. Also, majorities expected their economic situation to improve in the future.

By overwhelming majorities, the three groups express foreign policy views that are in line with U.S. government policies or American public opinion. They manifest no tendency to favor their "homeland" over the United States and they express neither affection for nor knowledge about Latin America in general. Indeed, each group is more positively oriented toward Great Britain than toward Latin America. Additionally, immigration issues have almost no salience for any of the groups, and none of the groups is particularly supportive of increased benefits for immigrants or refugees.

Nonetheless, Latino support for core American values is less clear. All the Latino groups voice greater trust in the government than Anglos do. Even though large majorities of Mexicans, Puerto Ricans, and Cubans express great patriotism, Anglos express higher levels of patriotism. Anglos are also more likely to indicate that individuals rather than government should take responsibility for housing, jobs, and income. These findings are somewhat surprising.[3]

Behaviorally, Mexicans, Puerto Ricans, and Cubans report different levels of participation in political and organizational activities. Mexicans and Puerto Ricans report lower interest in current events and vote at much lower levels than Cubans and Anglos, who report almost identical participation in both of these types of activities. Cubans, however, are much less active regarding political activities other than voting, and sometimes Mexicans report higher involvement than Anglos in nonelectoral arenas. Also, all groups report relatively high involvement in school-related activities.

Mexicans, Puerto Ricans, and Cubans do not report high rates of involvement in activities related to their respective groups. They do not have much knowledge about Latino leaders or organizations, but they express ethnic solidarity and support for co-ethnics. They also indicate a strong predisposition to vote for a co-ethnic if they have the opportunity to do so.

What does all this mean? Most significantly, that these groups defy simple categorization. On many key domestic issues, significant majorities of each group take the liberal position. On other issues, there is no consensus and, depending on the issue, Mexicans may be on the right, while Cubans and many Puerto Ricans are on the left of the nation's current political spectrum. Thus, labels such as liberal or conservative do not adequately describe the complexity of any one group's political views.

Overall, these groups do not constitute a political community. They clearly agree on some key questions, but they disagree on others. Indeed, sometimes a particular group more closely resembles Anglos than any one of the other Latino populations. This is especially evident regarding foreign policy.

Relatedly, and somewhat surprisingly, the respondents express higher affect toward Anglos than toward other Latinos. Their positive views on their experiences with government and their optimism about their future suggest that the relationship between these groups and mainstream society is not so harsh as to isolate the "Hispanic" community and make it easily mobilized around narrow ethnic appeals.

Taken together as a Hispanic population, then, they do not fit neatly within either the Democratic or the Republican parties. Nonetheless, if it were necessary to locate Hispanics as a single population within the party structure as it currently exists, their policy preferences would better fit under the Democratic umbrella.

These results also indicate that these groups are well within the mainstream of the nation's politics. There is no evidence here of values, demands, or behaviors that threaten the nation's cultural or political identity. In only one policy area, bilingual education, are Mexican, Puerto Rican, and Cuban views sufficiently coherent and distinct to constitute a distinct public policy. As has been indicated, however, the three groups overwhelmingly agree that the objective of bilingual education is to teach either English or English and Spanish. Thus, even on this issue, their views do not challenge the mainstream.

F. Conclusion

We have been surprised by many of our results. In future volumes, we will analyze our findings much more thoroughly and perhaps find explanations for some of these unexpected results. Until then, these data should be useful to anyone who wants answers to many of the basic questions that are regularly asked about Latinos.

These data describe how Mexicans, Puerto Ricans, and Cubans think and act today. Armed with this information, Latino leaders and others who would have a political relationship with Hispanics will be able to articulate more accurately and effectively the concerns of these groups and develop strategies to empower them further. We hope this information will also be valuable to those who have a vision of what Latino politics should be. Finally, we especially hope that our results will contribute to silencing uninformed critics who wrap their bigotry in false information.

Notes

1. Throughout this volume, we use the terms "Latino" and "Hispanic" interchangeably to refer to residents of the United States who can trace their ancestry to the Spanish-speaking regions of Latin America and the Caribbean. For reasons that we will discuss later in this chapter, Latinos in the Latino National Political Survey are residents of the United States who can trace their ancestry to Mexico, Puerto Rico, or Cuba.

We also use two other sets of racial/ethnic identification terms interchangeably—black or African American and white or Anglo.

2. Two Puerto Rican respondents were not born in either the continental United States or in Puerto Rico. As noncitizens, they are excluded from the analysis in chapters 3 through 9.

3. It must be noted that when these patterns are analyzed using advanced statistical techniques, the results indicate that there are no statistically significant differences between the Latino nationality groups and Anglos. That is, Mexicans, Puerto Ricans, and Cubans, per se, are not less patriotic or less supportive of economic individualism (de la Garza et al. 1992b). In other words, poor Mexicans and poor Anglos are comparably patriotic and equally supportive of government's providing jobs after other factors such as education and income are considered.

References

Bean, Frank D., and Marta Tienda. 1987. The Hispanic Population of the United States. New York: Russell Sage Foundation.

Caplan, Barbara. 1987. "Linking Cultural Characteristics to Political Opinion." In Rodolfo O. de la Garza, ed., Ignored Voices: Public Opinion Polls and the Latino Community, pp. 158-169. Austin: Center for Mexican American Studies Publications, University of Texas Press.

Chavez, Linda. 1991. Out of the Barrio: Toward a New Politics of Hispanic Assimilation. New York: Basic Books.

de la Garza, Rodolfo O. 1992. "Immigration Reforms as a Civil Rights Issue: A Mexican American Perspective," In Gillian Peel and Bruce Cain, eds., Developments in American Politics, pp. 309-322. New York: Oxford University Press.

———(ed.). 1987. Ignored Voices: Public Opinion Polls and the Latino Community. Austin: Center for Mexican American Studies Publications, University of Texas Press.

de la Garza, Rodolfo O., and Louis DeSipio. 1992. From Rhetoric to Reality: Latinos and the 1988 Elections. Boulder, CO: Westview Press.

de la Garza, Rodolfo O.; Angelo Falcon; F. Chris Garcia; and John Garcia. Forthcoming. "Mexican Immigrants, Mexican Americans and American Political Culture." In B. Edmonston and J. Passel, eds., Immigration and Ethnicity: The Integration of America's Newest Immigrants. Washington, DC: Urban Institute Press.

———. 1992c. "Mexican Puerto Rican and Cuban Foreign Policy Perspectives: A Test of Competing Explanations." Paper presented at the Annual Meetings of the Western Political Science Association, San Francisco, March.

———. 1992b. "Will the Real Americans Please Stand Up: A Comparison of Mexican,

Puerto Rican, Cuban and Anglo Political Values in the United States." Paper presented at the Center for American Political Studies, Department of Government, Harvard University. (Revised version of a paper by the same title presented at the Annual Meetings of the American Political Science Association, 1991).

―――.*1992a. "The Effects of Ethnicity on Political Culture: A Comparison of Puerto Rican and Anglo Political Values." Paper presented at the Workshop on Race, Ethnicity and Governance at the Center for American Political Studies, Department of Government, Harvard University.*

de la Garza, Rodolfo O., and Armando Trujillo. 1991. *"Latinos and the Official English Debate in the United States: Language Is Not the Issue." In David Schneiderman, ed.,* Language and the State: The Law and Politics of Identity, *pp. 209-226. Cowansville, Quebec: Les Editions Yvon Blais.*

DeSipio, Louis, and James Henson. 1992. *"The Cuban American Enclave and the Construction of Ethnicity." Paper presented at the annual meetings of the Midwest Political Science Association. Chicago, April.*

Falcon, Angelo; Rodolfo O. de la Garza; F. Chris Garcia; and John A. Garcia. 1991. *"Modes of Political Participation of Mexican Americans, Puerto Ricans and Cuban Americans: Preliminary Data from the Latino National Political Survey." Paper presented at the Annual Meeting of the American Political Science Association, Washington, September.*

Fuchs, Lawrence H. 1990. The American Kaleidoscope: Race Ethnicity and the Civic Culture. *Hanover, NH: Wesleyan University Press.*

Garcia, F. Chris. 1987. *"Comments on Papers Presented by the Panel on Latinos and the 1984 Elections." In Rodolfo O. de la Garza, ed.,* Ignored Voices: Public Opinion Polls and the Latino Community, *pp. 106-117. Austin: Center for Mexican American Studies Publications, University of Texas Press.*

Garcia, F. Chris; Rodolfo O. de la Garza; John A. Garcia; and Angelo Falcon. 1992. *"The Effects of Ethnicity on Partisanship, and Partisanship's Impact on Ethnicity: The Case of Mexicans, Puerto Ricans, Cubans and Anglos in the United States." Paper presented at the Annual Meetings of the Western Political Science Association, San Francisco, March.*

Garcia, F. Chris; John Garcia; Angelo Falcon; and Rodolfo O. de la Garza. 1992. Latino Politics: A Research Bibliography. *Austin: Center for Mexican American Studies Publications, University of Texas Press.*

―――.*1989. "Studying Latino Politics: The Development of the Latino National Political Survey." PS: Political Science and Politics 22: 848-852.*

Garcia, F. Chris; Rodolfo O. de la Garza; John A. Garcia; and Angelo Falcon. 1991. *"Ethnicity and Ideology: Political Attitudes of Mexicans, Puerto Ricans and Cubans." Paper presented at the Annual Meeting of the American Political Science Association, Washington, September.*

Garcia, John A.; F. Chris Garcia; Angelo Falcon and Rodolfo O. de la Garza. 1991. *"Ethnicity and National-Origin Status: Patterns of Identities among Latinos in the U.S." Paper presented at the Annual Meeting of the American Political Science Association. Washington, DC, September.*

Grenier, Guillermo. 1991. *"Los Bravos de la Pelicula: Politics and Cubans in Miami." Report to the Political Ethnography Project. University of Texas. Austin. [Forthcoming in de la Garza, Rodolfo O.; Martha Menchaca; and Louis DeSipio, eds.* Latinos and the 1990 Elections. *Boulder, CO: Westview Press.]*

National Association of Latino Elected Officials (NALEO) Educational Fund. 1992. The Latino Vote in 1992. *NALEO Background Paper 1992. Washington, DC: NALEO Educational Fund.*

————. 1991. National Roster of Hispanic Elected Officials 1991. *Washington, DC: NALEO Educational Fund.*

————. 1989. The National Latino Immigrant Survey. *Washington, DC: NALEO Educational Fund.*

Pachon, Harry P., and Louis DeSipio. 1992. *"Latino Elected Officials in the 1990s."* PS: Political Science and Politics 25 (2): 212-217.

Smith, Tom. 1990. *"Ethnic Survey."* GSS Topical Report Number 19. *National Opinion Research Center. Chicago: University of Chicago.*

U.S. Bureau of the Census, Current Population Reports. 1991a. Voting and Registration in the Election of November 1990. *Series P-20, No. 453. Washington, DC: U.S. Government Printing Office.*

————. 1991b. The Hispanic Population in the United States: *March 1990. Series P-20, No. 449. Washington, DC: U.S. Government Printing Office.*

2

Social and Demographic Characteristics of Native- and Foreign-Born Respondents

This chapter presents a portrait of the respondents to the Latino National Political Survey. These data allow the interested reader to make comparisons with census data so as to evaluate the sample. They also provide the background information for evaluating the characteristics of the people whose attitudes and behaviors we describe in other chapters of this volume. We examine the differences, if any, between the native-born (those born in the United States) and the foreign-born (those born in Mexico, Puerto Rico, or Cuba). We divide our analysis into six components: (1) personal and familial demographic characteristics; (2) education, income, and employment; (3) religion; (4) identity; (5) language abilities; and (6) immigration and citizenship status.

A. Personal and Familial Demographic Characteristics
(Tables 2.1–2.8)

Findings

Slightly more than half of the LNPS respondents were women (Table 2.1). Among the national-origin groups, 56 percent of Puerto Ricans, 52 percent of Anglos, 51 percent of Cubans, and 48 percent of Mexicans were women. Foreign-born men outnumbered foreign-born women; this was especially true among Mexicans.

Overwhelmingly, regardless of nativity, Cubans identified themselves racially as white (Table 2.2). Majorities of native-born Mexicans and foreign-born Puerto Ricans also identified racially as white. The majority of foreign-born Mexicans and 47 percent of native-born Puerto Ricans, on the other hand, used a Latino referent, such as Latino, Hispano, or Mexicano, as their racial identification.

Mexicans were the youngest of the respondents (Table 2.3). Fifty-four percent were thirty-four years old or younger. Foreign-born Mexicans were slightly younger than the native-born. Among Latinos, Cuban respondents were the oldest. Forty-one percent of Cubans were fifty-one years of age or older. Foreign-born Cubans are much older on average than the native-born.

The majority of Anglo, Cuban, and Mexican respondents were married (Table 2.4). Among Mexicans, nativity made little difference to the likelihood of being married. Among Cubans, the foreign-born were much more likely to be married.

Slightly fewer than 40 percent of Puerto Ricans were married. Another 20 percent were either separated or divorced. The native-born were much less likely than the foreign-born to be married.

More than 70 percent of Mexicans, Puerto Ricans, and Anglos had children or were legal guardians (Table 2.5). Approximately 55 percent of Cubans were parents or legal guardians. Among Mexicans, nativity had no effect on the likelihood of being a parent. For both Puerto Ricans and Cubans, the foreign-born were 15 percent to 20 percent more likely to be parents than were the native-born.

The majority of Mexicans, Cubans, and foreign-born Puerto Ricans who were married were married to co-ethnics (Table 2.6). Among native-born Latinos who were not married to co-ethnics, there was more likelihood of marriage to an Anglo than to a Latino who was not a co-ethnic.

The modal household size for Mexicans and Puerto Ricans was five or more, three for Cubans, and two for Anglos (Table 2.7). Among Mexicans, however, more than one-half of the foreign-born had households of five or more, compared with one-third of the native-born households. In general, households in which the respondent was foreign-born were larger than households in which the respondent was native-born.

Puerto Ricans were more likely than Cubans, Mexicans, or Anglos to rent their homes (Table 2.8). Native-born Mexicans and Anglos were the most likely to own their own homes.

Questions Asked

2, 3, 8, 9, 10, 11, 29, 30, and 180 (see Appendix 1).

TABLE 2.1 Gender, by National Origin and Nativity

Gender	Mexican		Puerto Rican		Cuban		Anglo	
	Foreign-Born	Native-Born	Foreign-Born	Native-Born	Foreign-Born	Native-Born	Foreign-Born	Native-Born
Female	310	429	223	105	303	43	15	223
	39.7%	56.1%	57.6%	51.7%	51.5%	47.3%	72.4%	51.3%
Male	471	336	164	98	285	48	6	212
	60.3%	43.9%	42.4%	48.3%	48.5%	52.7%	27.6%	48.7%
Total	781	765	387	202	587	92	21	435
	100.0%	100.0%	100.0%	100.0%	100.0%	100.0%	100.0%	100.0%

Note: For data on U.S. citizens, see Table 3.1.

TABLE 2.2 Race, by National Origin and Nativity

Race	Mexican		Puerto Rican		Cuban		Anglo	
	Foreign-Born	Native-Born	Foreign-Born	Native-Born	Foreign-Born	Native-Born	Foreign-Born	Native-Born
White	344	403	234	93	543	75	21	435
	46.9%	55.4%	62.9%	48.8%	93.5%	82.4%	100.0%	100.0%
Black	2	2	14	9	13	9	0	0
	0.2%	0.3%	3.9%	4.7%	2.2%	10.2%	0.0%	0.0%
Latino referent	389	323	124	89	25	7	0	0
	52.9%	44.3%	33.2%	46.5%	4.3%	7.4%	0.0%	0.0%
Total	735	728	372	191	581	91	21	435
	100.0%	100.0%	100.0%	100.0%	100.0%	100.0%	100.0%	100.0%

Note: For data on U.S. citizens, see Table 3.2.

TABLE 2.3   Age, by National Origin and Nativity

Age (years)	Mexican		Puerto Rican		Cuban		Anglo	
	Foreign-Born	Native-Born	Foreign-Born	Native-Born	Foreign-Born	Native-Born	Foreign-Born	Native-Born
18-24	171	179	40	80	39	47	7	54
	22.0%	23.4%	10.4%	39.5%	6.6%	51.7%	31.8%	12.3%
25-34	274	208	83	87	106	21	0	103
	35.2%	27.2%	21.5%	43.0%	18.3%	23.1%	1.5%	23.8%
35-50	235	186	157	30	172	12	3	123
	30.2%	24.4%	40.6%	14.6%	29.5%	12.8%	15.5%	28.3%
51-65	73	135	73	1	160	3	3	68
	9.3%	17.7%	19.0%	0.3%	27.4%	3.5%	13.9%	15.7%
66+	26	56	33	5	106	8	8	87
	3.4%	7.3%	8.6%	2.6%	18.2%	9.0%	37.4%	19.9%
Total	780	764	387	202	583	92	21	434
	100.0%	100.0%	100.0%	100.0%	100.0%	100.0%	100.0%	100.0%

Note: For data on U.S. citizens, see Table 3.3.

TABLE 2.4   Marital Status, by National Origin and Nativity

Marital Status	Mexican		Puerto Rican		Cuban		Anglo	
	Foreign-Born	Native-Born	Foreign-Born	Native-Born	Foreign-Born	Native-Born	Foreign-Born	Native-Born
Married	468	438	182	50	364	34	13	260
	60.6%	58.0%	47.6%	24.9%	63.0%	37.7%	63.5%	60.1%
Living with someone	70	53	31	26	12	0	0	25
	9.1%	7.0%	8.1%	13.0%	2.1%	0.0%	0.0%	5.7%
Separated or divorced	58	79	85	42	93	8	1	50
	7.5%	10.5%	22.3%	20.9%	16.2%	9.4%	6.2%	11.7%
Widowed	26	32	23	0	46	3	0	30
	3.4%	4.2%	6.0%	0.0%	8.0%	3.0%	2.3%	7.0%
Single	149	153	61	82	62	44	6	67
	19.4%	20.3%	16.0%	41.2%	10.7%	49.9%	28.1%	15.5%
Total	771	754	381	200	578	89	21	432
	100.0%	100.0%	100.0%	100.0%	100.0%	100.0%	100.0%	100.0%

Note: For data on U.S. citizens, see Table 3.4.

TABLE 2.5 Parent or Legal Guardian, by National Origin and Nativity

Respondent a Parent or Legal Guardian	Mexican		Puerto Rican		Cuban		Anglo	
	Foreign-Born	Native-Born	Foreign-Born	Native-Born	Foreign-Born	Native-Born	Foreign-Born	Native-Born
Yes	559	547	299	119	343	37	11	310
	71.8%	71.8%	77.3%	59.0%	58.4%	40.3%	55.4%	71.2%
No	219	214	88	83	244	55	9	125
	28.2%	28.2%	22.7%	41.0%	41.6%	59.7%	44.6%	28.8%
Total	778	761	387	202	587	92	20	435
	100.0%	100.0%	100.0%	100.0%	100.0%	100.0%	100.0%	100.0%

Note: For data on U.S. citizens, see Table 3.5.

TABLE 2.6 National Origin of Spouse, by National Origin and Nativity of Respondent

National Origin of Spouse	Mexican		Puerto Rican		Cuban	
	Foreign-Born	Native-Born	Foreign-Born	Native-Born	Foreign-Born	Native-Born
Mexican	478	341	18	7	11	0
	91.8%	74.9%	9.1%	10.9%	3.1%	0.0%
Cuban	1	0	4	0	304	17
	0.1%	0.1%	2.3%	0.0%	84.9%	70.7%
Puerto Rican	4	4	156	28	14	0
	0.8%	0.8%	79.0%	42.6%	3.8%	0.0%
Other Latino	9	10	14	3	17	0
	1.8%	2.3%	7.3%	4.6%	4.6%	0.0%
Anglo	29	100	5	28	13	7
	5.5%	22.0%	2.3%	41.9%	3.6%	29.3%
Total	521	456	197	67	358	24
	100.0%	100.0%	100.0%	100.0%	100.0%	100.0%

Note: For data on U.S. citizens, see Table 3.6.

TABLE 2.7 Household Size, by National Origin and Nativity

Number in Household	Mexican		Puerto Rican		Cuban		Anglo	
	Foreign-Born	Native-Born	Foreign-Born	Native-Born	Foreign-Born	Native-Born	Foreign-Born	Native-Born
One	26	40	41	16	61	6	1	64
	3.3%	5.3%	10.7%	7.7%	10.4%	6.2%	6.2%	14.8%
Two	74	138	67	44	146	13	10	174
	9.5%	18.1%	17.5%	22.0%	25.0%	14.7%	50.4%	39.9%
Three	115	160	80	44	142	25	4	77
	14.7%	20.9%	20.7%	21.8%	24.2%	26.9%	18.5%	17.7%
Four	155	191	66	45	114	35	2	54
	19.9%	25.0%	17.2%	22.4%	19.6%	38.1%	10.8%	12.4%
Five or more	410	235	130	53	122	13	3	66
	52.6%	30.7%	33.8%	26.1%	20.8%	14.2%	14.2%	15.2%
Total	780	764	384	201	584	92	21	435
	100.0%	100.0%	100.0%	100.0%	100.0%	100.0%	100.0%	100.0%

Note: For data on U.S. citizens, see Table 3.8.

TABLE 2.8 Tenancy, by National Origin and Nativity

Tenancy	Mexican		Puerto Rican		Cuban		Anglo	
	Foreign-Born	Native-Born	Foreign-Born	Native-Born	Foreign-Born	Native-Born	Foreign-Born	Native-Born
Rent	459	272	297	119	304	24	5	116
	58.9%	35.7%	76.8%	58.8%	51.7%	26.0%	26.2%	28.2%
Live with parents who own	19	58	4	25	27	21	0	0
	2.4%	7.6%	1.0%	12.5%	4.5%	23.4%	0.0%	0.0%
Own	239	367	58	20	216	26	13	263
	30.7%	48.2%	15.0%	9.9%	36.8%	27.9%	73.8%	63.9%
Other living arrange- ments	63	65	28	38	41	21	0	33
	8.1%	8.5%	7.1%	18.8%	6.9%	22.6%	0.0%	8.0%
Total	779	763	387	202	587	92	18	412
	100.0%	100.0%	100.0%	100.0%	100.0%	100.0%	100.0%	100.0%

Note: For data on U.S. citizens, see Table 3.9.

B. Education, Income, and Employment (Tables 2.9–2.22)

Findings

Foreign-born respondents had less education than the native-born, regardless of national origin (Table 2.9). More than 60 percent of foreign-born Mexicans, 40 percent of foreign-born Puerto Ricans, and 37 percent of foreign-born Cubans had no more than eight years of formal education.

Regardless of nativity, more than three-quarters of the Mexicans and the Puerto Ricans attended public schools (Table 2.10). The majority of Cubans also attended public schools exclusively; however, 32 percent of the foreign-born and 47 percent of the native-born Cubans attended private or parochial schools for part or all of their education.

Spouses of foreign-born respondents had lower levels of education than did spouses of native-born respondents (Table 2.11). Spouses of foreign-born Mexicans had the lowest levels of formal education of any of the spouses.

Combined household education levels suggest that levels of formal education are not consistent between spouses (Table 2.12). Particularly among the foreign-born, many respondents had a different level of education from their spouses.

The majority of Mexicans and Cubans, regardless of nativity, had not participated in bilingual education programs (Table 2.13). A majority of Puerto Ricans had taken bilingual education courses.

The parents of foreign-born respondents had lower average levels of formal education than did the parents of native-born respondents (Table 2.14). This was particularly true among Mexican respondents. Slightly more than 15 percent of Mexicans, 20 percent of Puerto Ricans, and 25 percent of Cubans had two parents with more than a high school education. At this level, nativity seems to be a less important determinant of parental education completed than does national origin.

Among all Latinos, and Mexicans in particular, the respondent's highest level of education completed does not seem to have been influenced by the level of education completed by the parent (Table 2.15).

On average, Mexican households had more wage earners than did Puerto Rican, Cuban, or Anglo households (Table 2.16).

Almost one-third of Puerto Rican households in which the respondent was foreign-born had no wage earners. This was also true of 17 percent of Cuban households where the respondent was foreign-born. This may be because the Cuban population is somewhat older and has a higher number of retirees (Table 2.21).

Despite having higher numbers of household members in the work force, households with a foreign-born respondent had lower incomes than did households with a native-born respondent (Table 2.17). More than half of households with a foreign-born Puerto Rican respondent had incomes of less than thirteen thousand dollars per year. At the other extreme, more than one-third of Cuban households with native-born respondents had incomes exceeding fifty thousand dollars per year.

Higher levels of income in the Cuban community become more evident with presentation of per capita income (Table 2.18). More than 22 percent of Cuban households with foreign-born respondents and almost one-third with native-born respondents had incomes of $10,001 to $20,000 per year for each household member. For the Mexican and Puerto Rican communities, the comparable rates were between 9 and 10 percent for the foreign-born and 20 and 21 percent for the native born.

Labor force participation rates vary by national origin and nativity. Almost three-quarters of native-born Cubans were in the work force, compared with just 47 percent of the foreign-born Puerto Ricans (Table 2.19).

While foreign-born Mexicans had higher labor force participation rates than their native-born co-ethnics, native-born Cubans and Puerto Ricans participated in the work force at higher rates than did their foreign-born co-ethnics.

Mexicans and Puerto Ricans in the work force are concentrated in blue-collar and service occupations (Table 2.20). Cuban respondents, particularly native-born Cuban respondents, were much more likely to be found in managerial, professional, technical, sales, or administrative support positions.

Mexicans and Puerto Ricans who were not in the labor force were most likely to be homemakers (Table 2.21). For Cubans, the most common reason given for not being in the labor force was retirement.

Only a handful of respondents, almost all native-born, have served in the military (Table 2.22).

Questions Asked

12, 13, 14, 15, 16, 17, 18, 19, 24, 25b, 26a, 26b, 31, 32, 166, 181, and 182.

TABLE 2.9 Education, by National Origin and Nativity

Education	Mexican		PuertoRican		Cuban		Anglo	
	Foreign-Born	Native-Born	Foreign-Born	Native-Born	Foreign-Born	Native-Born	Foreign-Born	Native-Born
0–8 years	476	135	157	19	220	4	0	4
	61.2%	17.7%	41.0%	9.5%	37.8%	4.9%	2.3%	1.0%
9–12 years, no degree	68	191	74	54	80	11	8	103
	8.7%	25.0%	19.4%	26.5%	13.8%	12.1%	37.3%	23.7%
High school diploma or GED	193	364	117	100	170	52	12	237
	24.7%	47.7%	30.5%	49.3%	29.2%	56.9%	56.1%	54.6%
Beyond high school	42	73	35	30	112	24	1	89
	5.4%	9.5%	9.2%	14.7%	19.3%	26.1%	4.4%	20.6%
Total	779	763	384	202	581	92	21	433
	100.0%	100.0%	100.0%	100.0%	100.0%	100.0%	100.0%	100.0%

Note: For data on U.S. citizens, see Table 3.10.

TABLE 2.10 Public or Private School Attendance, by National Origin and Nativity

Type of Education	Mexican		Puerto Rican		Cuban	
	Foreign-Born	Native-Born	Foreign-Born	Native-Born	Foreign-Born	Native-Born
Only public school	649	594	360	169	392	48
	83.3%	78.3%	93.1%	83.5%	66.8%	52.6%
Combination of public and private	55	106	7	26	97	26
	7.0%	14.0%	1.8%	13.0%	16.5%	27.9%
Only private school	32	33	10	7	93	17
	4.1%	4.3%	2.6%	3.5%	15.9%	19.0%
No formal education	44	26	10	0	5	0
	5.6%	3.4%	2.6%	0.0%	0.8%	0.5%
Total	779	759	387	202	587	92
	100.0%	100.0%	100.0%	100.0%	100.0%	100.0%

TABLE 2.11 Education of Spouse, by Respondent's National Origin and
Nativity

Education of Spouse	Mexican		Puerto Rican		Cuban	
	Foreign-Born	Native-Born	Foreign-Born	Native-Born	Foreign-Born	Native-Born
0–8 years	293	109	72	12	127	4
	37.5%	14.2%	18.7%	6.1%	21.6%	4.8%
9–11 years	66	115	45	20	36	6
	8.4%	15.0%	11.6%	10.1%	6.1%	6.2%
12 years	85	161	61	26	111	12
	10.9%	21.1%	15.8%	12.6%	19.0%	13.4%
Beyond high school	338	380	208	144	313	69
	43.3%	49.6%	53.9%	71.1%	53.3%	75.6%
Total	781	765	387	202	587	92
	100.0%	100.0%	100.0%	100.0%	100.0%	100.0%

TABLE 2.12 Combined Household Education Level, by Respondent's National
Origin and Nativity

Combined Education of Respondent and Spouse	Mexican		Puerto Rican		Cuban	
	Foreign-Born	Native-Born	Foreign-Born	Native-Born	Foreign-Born	Native-Born
Both 8 years or less	238	62	51	7	88	2
	30.5%	8.1%	13.4%	3.5%	15.2%	2.5%
One 8 years or less, one 9–12 years	114	71	42	11	54	2
	14.6%	9.3%	11.0%	5.2%	9.4%	2.4%
Both 9–12 years	76	225	67	37	94	18
	9.7%	29.4%	17.4%	18.5%	16.2%	19.6%
One beyond high school, one 8 years or less	179	49	84	7	116	2
	23.0%	6.5%	22.0%	3.4%	19.9%	2.4%
One beyond high school, one 9–12 years	145	311	120	114	153	43
	18.6%	40.8%	31.4%	56.3%	26.3%	47.1%
Both high school and above	28	45	18	26	76	24
	3.5%	5.9%	4.8%	13.0%	13.0%	26.1%
Total	779	763	384	202	581	92
	100.0%	100.0%	100.0%	100.0%	100.0%	100.0%

TABLE 2.13 Participation in Bilingual Education, by National Origin and Nativity

Participation in a Bilingual Education Program?	Mexican		Puerto Rican		Cuban	
	Foreign-Born	Native-Born	Foreign-Born	Native-Born	Foreign-Born	Native-Born
Yes	319	257	195	101	202	36
	41.2%	34.1%	50.9%	50.5%	34.7%	40.2%
No	456	497	189	99	380	54
	58.8%	65.9%	49.1%	49.5%	65.3%	59.8%
Total	775	754	384	200	582	90
	100.0%	100.0%	100.0%	100.0%	100.0%	100.0%

TABLE 2.14 Education of Respondent's Parents, by Respondent's National Origin and Nativity

Combined Parental Education Levels	Mexican		Puerto Rican		Cuban	
	Foreign-Born	Native-Born	Foreign-Born	Native-Born	Foreign-Born	Native-Born
Both 8 years or less	480	274	155	47	213	9
	61.5%	35.9%	40.1%	23.4%	36.3%	9.9%
One 8 years or less, one 9–12 years	46	87	26	32	52	17
	5.9%	11.3%	6.8%	15.8%	8.8%	18.0%
Both 9–12 years	22	118	21	36	56	17
	2.8%	15.4%	5.4%	17.9%	9.5%	18.4%
One beyond high school, one 8 years or less	82	99	66	17	67	7
	10.5%	13.0%	17.1%	8.4%	11.4%	7.9%
One beyond high school, one 9–12 years	7	58	15	26	49	16
	0.9%	7.5%	4.0%	12.7%	8.4%	17.1%
Both beyond high school	143	129	103	44	151	26
	18.4%	16.8%	26.7%	21.8%	25.6%	28.8%
Total	781	765	387	202	587	92
	100.0%	100.0%	100.0%	100.0%	100.0%	100.0%

TABLE 2.15 Parents' Education, by Respondent's National Origin and
Educational Attainment

Combined Parental Education Levels	Mexican Education Completed		Puerto Rican Education Completed		Cuban Education Completed	
	0-12 Years/ No HS Degree	HS Degree or Beyond	0-12 Years/ No HS Degree	HS Degree or Beyond	0-12 Years/ No HS Degree	HS Degree or Beyond
Both 8 years or less	470	283	107	94	119	102
	54.0%	42.2%	35.2%	33.4%	37.8%	28.6%
One 8 years or less, one 9–12 years	37	96	19	38	20	47
	4.2%	14.4%	6.3%	13.4%	6.2%	13.2%
Both 9–12 years	43	97	15	42	22	50
	4.9%	14.5%	4.9%	14.9%	6.9%	13.8%
One beyond high school, one 8 years or less	113	69	46	38	41	32
	12.9%	10.2%	15.0%	13.3%	13.1%	9.1%
One beyond high school, one 9–12 years	16	47	9	32	17	46
	1.9%	7.0%	2.8%	11.5%	5.4%	12.8%
Both beyond high school	192	79	109	38	96	80
	22.1%	11.8%	35.7%	13.5%	30.6%	22.4%
Total	871	671	304	281	315	358
	100.0%	100.0%	100.0%	100.0%	100.0%	100.0%

TABLE 2.16 Household Wage Earners, by National Origin and Nativity

Salaried Workers	Mexican		Puerto Rican		Cuban		Anglo	
	Foreign-Born	Native-Born	Foreign-Born	Native-Born	Foreign-Born	Native-Born	Foreign-Born	Native-Born
None	27	74	114	30	99	7	8	74
	3.5%	9.7%	29.4%	14.7%	16.9%	7.9%	37.4%	17.1%
One	223	206	126	77	180	13	5	142
	28.5%	26.9%	32.7%	38.0%	30.7%	14.2%	21.9%	33.0%
Two	274	305	106	58	201	40	3	166
	35.1%	39.8%	27.5%	28.7%	34.3%	43.7%	16.1%	38.5%
Three	100	131	32	26	76	22	3	37
	12.8%	17.1%	8.4%	13.0%	13.0%	24.5%	14.2%	8.7%
Four	72	39	3	10	18	7	2	9
	9.3%	5.1%	0.8%	5.0%	3.2%	8.1%	10.4%	2.2%
Five or more	84	10	5	1	11	2	0	2
	10.8%	1.3%	1.3%	0.7%	2.0%	1.8%	0.0%	0.6%
Total	780	765	387	202	586	92	21	431
	100.0%	100.0%	100.0%	100.0%	100.0%	100.0%	100.0%	100.0%

Note: For data on U.S. citizens, see Table 3.11.

TABLE 2.17 Household Income, by National Origin and Nativity

Household Income	Mexican		Puerto Rican		Cuban		Anglo	
	Foreign-Born	Native-Born	Foreign-Born	Native-Born	Foreign-Born	Native-Born	Foreign-Born	Native-Born
$0–$12,999	219	183	181	66	169	11	9	79
	30.9%	25.3%	51.3%	34.7%	32.1%	12.7%	44.6%	19.5%
$13,000–$19,999	136	124	55	37	105	7	2	50
	19.2%	17.1%	15.7%	19.4%	19.9%	7.6%	8.3%	12.3%
$20,000–$29,999	161	136	57	37	100	22	4	98
	22.6%	18.8%	16.1%	19.7%	19.1%	24.6%	20.0%	24.1%
$30,000–$39,999	88	133	36	26	61	14	1	66
	12.4%	18.4%	10.3%	13.6%	11.6%	15.5%	3.1%	16.3%
$40,000–$49,999	55	69	11	12	25	2	3	40
	7.8%	9.5%	3.1%	6.0%	4.7%	2.7%	13.0%	9.7%
$50,000 or more	51	79	12	13	66	33	2	74
	7.1%	11.0%	3.5%	6.7%	12.6%	36.9%	10.9%	18.1%
Total	710	724	352	191	526	89	21	407
	100.0%	100.0%	100.0%	100.0%	100.0%	100.0%	100.0%	100.0%

Note: For data on U.S. citizens, see Table 3.12.

TABLE 2.18 Per Capita Household Income, by National Origin and Nativity

Per Capita Annual Household Income	Mexican		Puerto Rican		Cuban		Anglo	
	Foreign-Born	Native-Born	Foreign-Born	Native-Born	Foreign-Born	Native-Born	Foreign-Born	Native-Born
$2,500 or less	164	129	109	47	69	4	0	20
	21.3%	17.1%	28.6%	23.5%	12.1%	3.8%	0.0%	4.8%
$2,501–$5,000	231	140	83	35	128	10	5	54
	30.1%	18.6%	21.9%	17.5%	22.5%	11.1%	25.6%	13.2%
$5,001–$10,000	226	242	119	58	179	28	8	106
	29.5%	32.1%	31.2%	28.8%	31.5%	30.5%	38.0%	26.0%
$10,001–$20,000	77	157	33	41	127	30	4	151
	10.1%	20.9%	8.6%	20.4%	22.2%	32.8%	21.7%	37.0%
$20,001 or more	12	55	6	9	22	17	3	77
	1.5%	7.3%	1.7%	4.5%	3.8%	18.7%	14.7%	19.0
Refused to answer	58	31	30	10	45	3	0	0
	7.5%	4.1%	8.0%	5.2%	7.9%	3.0%	0.0%	0.0%
Total	768	754	380	200	570	92	21	407
	100.0%	100.0%	100.0%	100.0%	100.0%	100.0%	100.0%	100.0%

Note: For data on U.S. citizens, see Table 3.13.

TABLE 2.19 Labor Force Status of Respondent, by National Origin and Nativity

Present Work Situation of Respondent	Mexican		Puerto Rican		Cuban		Anglo	
	Foreign-Born	Native-Born	Foreign-Born	Native-Born	Foreign-Born	Native-Born	Foreign-Born	Native-Born
In labor force	543	460	183	112	346	68	8	282
	69.8%	60.3%	47.3%	55.2%	59.0%	74.6%	36.3%	65.1%
Temporarily unemployed	78	90	41	30	38	9	0	23
	10.1%	11.8%	10.6%	15.0%	6.6%	10.1%	0.7%	5.3%
Not in labor force	157	212	162	60	202	14	13	128
	20.2%	27.8%	42.1%	29.7%	34.4%	15.3%	63.0%	29.6%
Total	779	763	386	202	586	92	21	433
	100.0%	100.0%	100.0%	100.0%	100.0%	100.0%	100.0%	100.0%

Note: For data on U.S. citizens, see Table 3.14.

TABLE 2.20 Occupation, by National Origin and Nativity

Occupation	Mexican		Puerto Rican		Cuban		Anglo	
	Foreign-Born	Native-Born	Foreign-Born	Native-Born	Foreign-Born	Native-Born	Foreign-Born	Native-Born
Managerial, professional, or specialty occupation	35	74	22	16	53	19	1	64
	4.6%	9.8%	5.6%	7.9%	9.1%	20.9%	5.3%	15.0%
Technical, sales, or administrative support	55	158	41	58	105	34	6	90
	7.2%	20.8%	10.6%	29.1%	18.0%	36.8%	30.1%	21.1%
Service	115	96	49	24	61	2	0	38
	15.0%	12.7%	12.7%	11.9%	10.4%	2.2%	0.4%	8.9%
Farming, forestry, or fishing	101	15	1	3	15	0	0	5
	13.2%	1.9%	0.2%	1.6%	2.5%	0.0%	0.0%	1.1%
Precision production or crafts	90	62	25	8	46	7	0	48
	11.8%	8.1%	6.4%	3.9%	7.9%	7.5%	0.0%	11.3%
Operator, fabricator, or laborer	199	112	67	23	84	14	0	39
	26.1%	14.8%	17.4%	11.6%	14.4%	15.5%	1.2%	9.2%
Not in labor force	168	242	182	68	220	16	13	142
	22.0%	31.9%	47.1%	34.0%	37.7%	17.2%	63.0%	33.4%
Total	763	758	386	200	585	92	21	427
	100.0%	100.0%	100.0%	100.0%	100.0%	100.0%	100.0%	100.0%

Note: For data on U.S. citizens, see Table 3.15.

TABLE 2.21 Reason for Not Being in the Work Force, by National Origin and
Nativity

Reason for Not Being in the Labor Force	Mexican		Puerto Rican		Cuban		Anglo	
	Foreign-Born	Native-Born	Foreign-Born	Native-Born	Foreign-Born	Native-Born	Foreign-Born	Native-Born
Unemployed	15	33	20	10	22	2	0	17
	8.7%	13.5%	10.9%	14.3%	9.8%	11.1%	0.0%	12.1%
Disabled	7	13	22	11	15	0	0	5
	4.4%	5.2%	11.8%	16.5%	7.0%	1.7%	0.0%	3.3%
Retired	24	79	44	5	96	8	7	91
	14.2%	32.6%	24.4%	8.1%	43.4%	49.4%	55.5%	64.0%
Homemaker	117	91	91	25	71	5	3	25
	70.0%	37.7%	49.8%	37.0%	32.3%	31.3%	19.5%	17.8%
Student	5	27	5	16	16	1	3	4
	2.7%	11.0%	3.0%	24.1%	7.5%	6.6%	25.1%	2.8%
Total	168	242	182	68	220	16	13	142
	100.0%	100.0%	100.0%	100.0%	100.0%	100.0%	100.0%	100.0%

Note: For data on U.S. citizens, see Table 3.16.

TABLE 2.22 Service in Armed Forces, by National Origin and Nativity

	Mexican		Puerto Rican		Cuban	
Military Service	Foreign-Born	Native-Born	Foreign-Born	Native-Born	Foreign-Born	Native-Born
Yes	15	98	22	8	4	13
	1.9%	12.8%	5.7%	4.1%	0.6%	13.7%
No	765	666	359	192	583	79
	98.1%	87.2%	94.3%	95.9%	99.4%	86.3%
Total	779	764	381	200	587	92
	100.0%	100.0%	100.0%	100.0%	100.0%	100.0%

C. Religion (Tables 2.23–2.26)

Findings

Among Latino respondents who had a religious affiliation, between 60 and 80 percent were Catholic (Table 2.23). The highest rates of Protestant affiliation occurred in the Puerto Rican community. One-quarter of the native-born Cubans, as well as 19 percent of the native-born Puerto Ricans and 11 percent of the native-born Mexicans, stated no religious preference or mentioned a non-Catholic and non-Protestant affiliation. These rates exceed the "no-preference" responses among the foreign-born, regardless of national origin.

In general, only 20 percent to 30 percent of all Latinos, compared to 34 percent of Anglos, had had born-again experiences (Table 2.24). The highest levels of born-again experiences occurred among foreign-born Puerto Ricans and the lowest among Cubans, regardless of nativity.

Mexicans, regardless of nativity, and the foreign-born in general, received the most guidance from religion (Table 2.25). Fewer than 10 percent of all respondents reported that they received no guidance from religion.

Despite the high levels of guidance received from religion, more than 40 percent of respondents, regardless of national origin or nativity, rarely or never attended religious services (Table 2.26). The highest rates of church attendance were among foreign-born Mexicans.

Questions Asked

20a, 20b, 21, 22, and 23.

TABLE 2.23   Religious Affiliation, by National Origin and Nativity

Religious Affiliation	Mexican		Puerto Rican		Cuban		Anglo	
	Foreign-Born	Native-Born	Foreign-Born	Native-Born	Foreign-Born	Native-Born	Foreign-Born	Native-Born
Catholic	638	557	263	121	469	59	6	91
	81.6%	73.1%	67.9%	59.9%	79.8%	63.9%	28.7%	20.9%
Protestant	66	118	89	42	84	9	7	239
	8.4%	15.5%	23.1%	20.7%	14.3%	10.2%	35.6%	55.0%
Other/no preference	78	87	35	39	34	24	7	105
	10.0%	11.4%	9.0%	19.4%	5.9%	25.9%	35.6%	24.1%
Total	781	762	387	202	587	92	21	435
	100.0%	100.0%	100.0%	100.0%	100.0%	100.0%	100.0%	100.0%

Note: For data on U.S. citizens, see Table 3.18.

TABLE 2.24 Born-Again Religious Experience, by National Origin and Nativity

Born-Again Religious Experience	Mexican		Puerto Rican		Cuban		Anglo	
	Foreign-Born	Native-Born	Foreign-Born	Native-Born	Foreign-Born	Native-Born	Foreign-Born	Native-Born
No	532	491	220	127	455	58	11	238
	73.2%	69.9%	61.2%	70.8%	81.5%	79.8%	79.6%	66.3%
Yes	195	211	140	53	103	15	3	121
	26.8%	30.1%	38.8%	29.2%	18.5%	20.2%	20.4%	33.7%
Total	727	702	360	180	558	73	14	359
	100.0%	100.0%	100.0%	100.0%	100.0%	100.0%	100.0%	100.0%

Note: For data on U.S. citizens, see Table 3.19.

TABLE 2.25 Religious Guidance, by National Origin and Nativity

Guidance Received from Religion	Mexican		Puerto Rican		Cuban		Anglo	
	Foreign-Born	Native-Born	Foreign-Born	Native-Born	Foreign-Born	Native-Born	Foreign-Born	Native-Born
None	42	40	25	11	51	5	0	25
	5.8%	5.6%	6.8%	6.0%	9.1%	6.2%	0.6%	6.9%
Some	237	226	85	91	158	31	6	140
	32.7%	32.2%	23.5%	50.6%	28.3%	42.4%	45.3%	38.8%
Quite a bit	210	216	134	39	172	21	5	75
	29.0%	30.8%	37.0%	21.7%	30.9%	28.0%	33.5%	20.9%
A great deal	235	220	118	39	177	17	3	121
	32.5%	31.3%	32.6%	21.7%	31.7%	23.4%	20.6%	33.5%
Total	725	702	362	180	558	73	14	362
	100.0%	100.0%	100.0%	100.0%	100.0%	100.0%	100.0%	100.0%

Note: For data on U.S. citizens, see Table 3.20.

TABLE 2.26 Attendance at Religious Services, by National Origin and Nativity

Attendance at Religious Services	Mexican		Puerto Rican		Cuban		Anglo	
	Foreign-Born	Native-Born	Foreign-Born	Native-Born	Foreign-Born	Native-Born	Foreign-Born	Native-Born
Never	318	360	166	61	169	42	12	196
	40.8%	47.0%	43.0%	30.4%	28.8%	46.3%	59.2%	45.5%
Almost never	15	22	25	21	66	4	0	29
	2.0%	2.8%	6.6%	10.2%	11.3%	4.2%	0.0%	6.8%
A few times a year	39	69	49	46	75	8	3	74
	5.0%	9.0%	12.6%	22.6%	12.8%	8.8%	15.1%	17.3%
Once/twice a month	221	176	78	40	169	25	4	90
	28.4%	23.0%	20.3%	19.8%	28.8%	27.8%	19.4%	20.9%
Almost every week	186	139	68	34	108	12	1	41
	23.9%	18.1%	17.6%	17.0%	18.3%	13.0%	6.2%	9.5%
Total	781	765	387	202	587	92	21	430
	100.0%	100.0%	100.0%	100.0%	100.0%	100.0%	100.0%	100.0%

Note: For data on U.S. citizens, see Table 3.21.

D. Identity (Table 2.27)

Findings

The identification that was used by the greatest numbers of LNPS respondents was a national-origin label (Table 2.27). National-origin identifications include such terms as Mexican American, Chicano, Puerto Rican, or Cuban. For all three groups, the second-most-common form of identification was found in pan-ethnic identifications such as Latino, Hispanic or Spanish American. The native-born of all groups are much more likely to use pan-ethnic labels. The second-most-common form of identification for native-born Cuban respondents was American.

Questions Asked

4 and 5.

TABLE 2.27 Preferred Ethnic Identification, by National Origin and Nativity

Ethnic Identification	Mexican Foreign-Born	Mexican Native-Born	Puerto Rican Foreign-Born	Puerto Rican Native-Born	Cuban Foreign-Born	Cuban Native-Born
Mexican origin	659	461	0	5	0	0
	85.6%	61.8%	0.0%	2.6%	0.0%	0.0%
Puerto Rican origin	2	0	324	113	4	0
	0.3%	0.0%	84.1%	56.7%	0.6%	0.0%
Cuban origin	0	0	2	0	476	36
	0.0%	0.0%	0.4%	0.0%	83.0%	40.6%
Pan-ethnic	106	212	49	39	68	18
	13.7%	28.4%	12.7%	19.4%	11.9%	20.1%
American	3	73	11	43	26	34
	0.3%	9.7%	2.8%	21.3%	4.5%	39.3%
Total	770	746	386	199	573	88
	100.0%	100.0%	100.0%	100.0%	100.0%	100.0%

Notes: For data on U.S. citizens, see Table 4.6.

Foreign-born Mexican respondents prefer to be identified as Mexican (82), Mexicano(a) (543), Mexican American (30), Chicano(a) (3), Puerto Rican (2), Hispanic (31), Latino(a) (29), Spanish (14), Spanish American (10), Hispano (21), and American (3). U.S.-born Mexicans prefer the following identity terms: Mexican (82), Mexicano(a) (44), Mexican-American (307), Chicano(a) (27), Hispanic (132), Latino(a) (10), Spanish (23), Spanish American (40), Raza (1), Hispano (8), and American (73).

Foreign-born Puerto Rican respondents prefer to use Cuban (2), Puerto Rican (324), Niuyorican (1), Hispanic (9), Latino(a) (4), Spanish (4), Spanish American (23), Hispano (9), and American (11). U.S.-born Puerto Ricans prefer Mexican (5), Puerto Rican (104), Niuyorican (9), Hispanic (11), Latino(a) (3), Spanish (4), Spanish American (19), Hispano (1), and American (43).

Among foreign-born Cuban respondents, the preferred identity terms are Cuban (476), Puerto Rican (4), Hispanic (9), Latino(a) (15), Spanish (5), Spanish American (24), Hispano (15), and American (26). U.S.-born Cubans prefer Cuban (36), Hispanic (12), Spanish (1), Spanish American (3), and American (34).

E. Language Abilities (Tables 2.28–2.31)

Findings

The majority of foreign-born Cubans and Mexicans used Spanish exclusively at home, compared to 30 percent of foreign-born Puerto Ricans (Table 2.28). Among the native-born, 62 percent of Mexicans, 50 percent of Puerto Ricans and 31 percent of Cubans used English predominantly or exclusively at home. Nearly one-third of native-born Cubans relied more on Spanish than on English as the home language.

Foreign-born respondents were stronger in Spanish and native-born respondents stronger in English (Table 2.29). More than two-thirds of native-born respondents, regardless of national origin, were better in English or spoke no Spanish. More national-origin variation existed among the foreign-born. Seventy-nine percent of foreign-born Mexicans and 74 percent of foreign-born Cubans were better in Spanish or only spoke Spanish. Among foreign-born Puerto Ricans, the percentage who used Spanish dominantly or exclusively dropped to 60 percent. Between 15 percent and 30 percent of respondents were equally capable in Spanish and English. The native-born were more likely to be fully bilingual than were the foreign-born.

Among respondents who answered the LNPS in Spanish, more than half of the foreign-born demonstrated high English literacy on a language test (Table 2.30). High English literacy rates among native-born respondents who answered the LNPS in Spanish ranged from 17 percent for Cubans to 40 percent for Mexicans.

Foreign-born respondents who answered the LNPS in English generally had low Spanish-language literacy rates (Table 2.31). For the native-born, the number with high Spanish literacy rates varied by national origin. More than half of native-born Mexicans who answered questions in English had high Spanish literacy. For Puerto Ricans, more than 40 percent had high English literacy. The rate for Cubans was 26 percent.

Questions Asked

168, 169, and SAQ2.

TABLE 2.28 Home Language of Respondent, by National Origin and Nativity

Language Spoken in Home	Mexican Foreign-Born	Mexican Native-Born	Puerto Rican Foreign-Born	Puerto Rican Native-Born	Cuban Foreign-Born	Cuban Native-Born
Only Spanish	408	22	117	9	334	7
	52.3%	2.8%	30.3%	4.5%	57.1%	7.6%
More Spanish than English	204	67	109	27	138	24
	26.2%	8.8%	28.3%	13.3%	23.6%	26.4%
Both languages	98	195	109	66	82	32
	12.6%	25.6%	28.3%	32.6%	14.0%	35.1%
More English than Spanish	47	250	40	49	15	15
	6.1%	32.7%	10.4%	24.5%	2.5%	16.5%
Only English	22	230	10	51	16	13
	2.9%	30.1%	2.7%	25.1%	2.7%	14.5%
Total	781	765	386	202	585	92
	100.0%	100.0%	100.0%	100.0%	100.0%	100.0%

Note: For data on U.S. citizens, see Table 4.9.

TABLE 2.29 Overall Language Ability, by National Origin and Nativity

Overall Language Ability	Mexican Foreign-Born	Mexican Native-Born	Puerto Rican Foreign-Born	Puerto Rican Native-Born	Cuban Foreign-Born	Cuban Native-Born
Only Spanish	147	4	44	0	142	0
	18.8%	0.5%	11.4%	0.0%	24.3%	0.0%
Better in Spanish	471	58	189	10	294	3
	60.3%	7.7%	48.9%	4.8%	50.0%	3.8%
No difference	112	186	91	56	96	26
	14.3%	24.3%	23.5%	27.5%	16.3%	28.6%
Better in English	50	453	63	121	53	57
	6.5%	59.2%	16.2%	59.7%	9.0%	62.5%
Only English	1	64	0	16	2	5
	0.2%	8.3%	0.1%	8.0%	0.4%	5.1%
Total	781	764	387	202	587	92
	100.0%	100.0%	100.0%	100.0%	100.0%	100.0%

Note: For data on U.S. citizens, see Table 4.8.

TABLE 2.30 English Literacy Among Respondents Interviewed in Spanish, by National Origin and Nativity

English Literacy Among the Spanish-Dominant	Mexican		Puerto Rican		Cuban	
	Foreign-Born	Native-Born	Foreign-Born	Native-Born	Foreign-Born	Native-Born
Low	249	66	132	28	193	18
	38.6%	60.2%	48.3%	77.9%	39.2%	82.8%
High	396	43	141	8	299	4
	61.4%	39.8%	51.7%	22.1%	60.8%	17.2%
Total	644	109	273	36	492	22
	100.0%	100.0%	100.0%	100.0%	100.0%	100.0%

Note: For data on U.S. citizens, see Table 4.10.

TABLE 2.31 Spanish Literacy Among Respondents Interviewed in English, by National Origin and Nativity

Spanish Literacy Among the English-Dominant	Mexican		Puerto Rican		Cuban	
	Foreign-Born	Native-Born	Foreign-Born	Native-Born	Foreign-Born	Native-Born
Low	118	325	86	97	80	50
	87.0%	49.5%	76.7%	58.3%	86.1%	73.8%
High	18	331	26	69	13	18
	13.0%	50.5%	23.3%	41.7%	13.9%	26.2%
Total	136	656	112	166	93	68
	100.0%	100.0%	100.0%	100.0%	100.0%	100.0%

Note: For data on U.S. citizens, see Table 4.11.

F. Immigration and Citizenship Status (Tables 2.32–2.34)

Findings

Puerto Ricans migrated to the United States at a younger age than either Mexicans or Cubans (Table 2.32). Fully 60 percent of Mexicans and 75 percent of Cubans migrated to the United States as adults.

The overwhelming majority of foreign-born Latino residents planned to stay in the United States permanently (Table 2.33). Just 6 percent of Cubans, 8 percent of Mexicans, and 24 percent of Puerto Ricans planned to return to their country of origin.

Despite their intent to stay in the United States, many Latino immigrants had not naturalized (Table 2.34). In both the Cuban and the Mexican immigrant communities, more immigrants desired U.S. citizenship than had actually completed the naturalization process. As noted in Chapter 1, Puerto Ricans born in Puerto Rico are U.S. citizens by birth.

Less than 20 percent of noncitizen Latino immigrants were undecided or had no plans to apply for naturalization. An equal percentage of Mexicans and Cubans did not plan to become U.S. citizens.

Questions Asked

40, 43, and 45.

TABLE 2.32 Age at Immigration, by National Origin

Age at Immigration (years)	Mexican	Puerto Rican	Cuban
1-6	60	73	51
	7.7%	18.9%	8.8%
7-18	251	121	98
	32.1%	31.4%	16.7%
18 or more	470	192	438
	60.2%	49.7%	74.6%
Total	781	386	587
	100.0%	100.0%	100.0%

TABLE 2.33 Foreign-Born Respondents' Intent to Stay in the United States, by National Origin

Respondent's Intention	Mexican	Puerto Rican	Cuban
Remain in U.S. permanently	511	203	320
	76.2%	56.2%	86.4%
Return to country of origin	56	88	21
	8.4%	24.4%	5.6%
Undecided	104	70	30
	15.4%	19.4%	8.0%
Total	671	361	370
	100.0%	100.0%	100.0%

TABLE 2.34 Citizenship Status of Foreign-Born, by National Origin

U.S. Citizenship Status	Mexican	Puerto Rican	Cuban	Anglo
U.S. citizen	113	385	220	10
	15.3%	99.4%	38.1%	50.1%
Desires U.S. citizenship	483	2	252	5
	65.1%	0.4%	43.7%	23.8%
No plans to apply	109	0	87	5
	14.7%	0.0%	15.0%	24.2%
Undecided	37	1	18	0
	4.9%	0.2%	3.2%	1.9%
Total	742	387	577	21
	100.0%	100.0%	100.0%	100.0%

3

Social and Demographic Characteristics of U.S. Citizens

In this chapter, we examine the social and demographic composition of U.S. citizen respondents (the population that we discuss in chapters 3 through 9 of this volume) to the Latino National Political Survey.

Our discussion revolves around three elements: (1) personal and familial demographic characteristics; (2) education, income, and employment; and (3) religion.

A. Personal and Familial Demographic Characteristics
(Tables 3.1–3.9)

Findings

Women were the majority of each group (Table 3.1).

Cubans identified themselves in racial terms differently from either Mexicans or Puerto Ricans (Table 3.2). More than 90 percent of Cubans saw themselves as white. While bare majorities in the other two Latino communities also identified as white, 43 percent of Mexicans and 38 percent of Puerto Ricans identified themselves racially as Latino, or some equivalent term.

The modal age category among Mexican respondents was from twenty-five to thirty-four; for Puerto Ricans and Anglos, thirty-five to fifty; and for Cubans, 51 to 65 (Table 3.3).

The majority of Mexican, Cuban, and Anglo respondents were married (Table 3.4). Among Puerto Ricans, almost 40 percent were married, more than 20 percent were separated or divorced, and almost 25 percent were single.

Of the four national-origin groups, Cubans were the least likely to be parents (Table 3.5).

Married Cuban respondents were the most likely to be married to co-ethnics (Table 3.6). Although the size of the majority is smaller, both Mexicans and Puerto Ricans were also more likely than not to be married to co-ethnics. Respondents were much more likely to be married to Anglos than to be married to Latinos who traced their ancestry to countries other than their own. One-fifth of Mexicans were married to Anglos.

Mexicans have a much longer history in the United States than either Cubans or Puerto Ricans (Table 3.7). Forty-two percent of Mexicans had two or more grandparents who were born in the United States. Among Mexicans and Puerto Ricans, just 6 percent were third-generation Americans.

Cuban and Anglo households were smaller than Mexican and Puerto Rican households (Table 3.8).

Tenancy patterns varied greatly between Latino national-origin groups. More than half of Mexican and Cuban respondents either owned their homes or lived with their parents, who owned (Table 3.9). Seven in ten Puerto Ricans, on the other hand, rented their homes. Overall, Anglos were more likely than any of the Latino national-origin groups to own their homes.

Questions Asked

2, 3, 8, 9, 10, 11, 20, 29, 33, 34, 35, 36, 37, 38, and 180.

TABLE 3.1 Gender, by National Origin

Gender	Mexican	Puerto Rican	Cuban	Anglo
Female	472	327	172	230
	53.7%	55.7%	55.1%	51.7%
Male	406	260	140	215
	46.3%	44.3%	44.9%	48.3%
Total	878	587	312	446
	100.0%	100.0%	100.0%	100.0%

TABLE 3.2 Race, by National Origin

Race	Mexican	Puerto Rican	Cuban	Anglo
White	470	326	285	446
	56.5%	58.1%	92.5%	100.0%
Black	2	23	11	0
	0.2%	4.2%	3.7	0.0%
Latino referent	360	211	12	0
	43.3%	37.7%	3.8%	0.0%
Total	832	560	308	446
	100.0%	100.0%	100.0%	100.0%

TABLE 3.3 Age, by National Origin

Age (years)	Mexican	Puerto Rican	Cuban	Anglo
18–24	194	119	55	58
	22.2%	20.3%	17.5%	13.0%
25–34	234	170	62	103
	26.7%	29.0%	20.0%	23.2%
35–50	226	186	68	123
	25.8%	31.6%	21.8%	27.6%
51–65	154	74	79	68
	17.5%	12.6%	25.4%	15.3%
66+	69	38	48	93
	7.9%	6.5%	15.3%	20.8%
Total	877	587	312	445
	100.0%	100.0%	100.0%	100.0%

TABLE 3.4 Marital Status, by National Origin

Marital Status	Mexican	Puerto Rican	Cuban	Anglo
Married	515	231	185	266
	59.4%	39.9%	60.2%	60.2%
Living with someone	55	56	1	25
	6.4%	9.7%	0.2%	5.6%
Separated or divorced	91	126	45	50
	10.5%	21.8%	14.6%	11.4%
Widowed	39	23	14	31
	4.5%	3.9%	4.6%	6.9%
Single	167	143	63	71
	19.3%	24.7%	20.4%	16.0%
Total	867	579	307	442
	100.0%	100.0%	100.0%	100.0%

TABLE 3.5 Parent or Legal Guardian, by National Origin

Respondent a Parent or Legal Guardian?	Mexican	Puerto Rican	Cuban	Anglo
Yes	628	418	162	316
	71.8%	71.2%	52.0%	71.0%
No	246	169	150	129
	28.2%	28.8%	48.0%	29.0%
Total	874	587	312	445
	100.0%	100.0%	100.0%	100.0%

TABLE 3.6 National Origin of Spouse, by National Origin of Respondent

National Origin of Spouse	Mexican	Puerto Rican	Cuban
Mexican	404	25	1
	76.1%	9.6%	0.8%
Cuban	0	4	144
	0.1%	1.5%	86.4%
Puerto Rican	4	184	7
	0.8%	69.9%	4.3%
Other Latino	13	18	2
	2.4%	6.7%	1.0%
Anglo	110	33	13
	20.6%	12.4%	7.6%
Total	531	263	166
	100.0%	100.0%	100.0%

TABLE 3.7 Generation in the United States, by National Origin

Nativity of Respondent, Parents, and Grandparents	Mexican	Puerto Rican	Cuban
Respondent foreign-born	113	385	220
	13.2%	65.7%	70.9%
Respondent U.S.-born and parents foreign-born	182	149	70
	21.2%	25.4%	22.4%
Respondent and one parent U.S.-born	93	16	3
	10.8%	2.7%	0.9%
Respondent and both parents U.S.-born	113	1	0
	13.2%	0.2%	0.0%
Respondent and both parents and two grandparents U.S.-born	207	35	17
	24.2%	6.0%	5.6%
Respondent and both parents and three or more grandparents U.S.-born	149	0	1
	17.4%	0.0%	0.2%
Total	857	585	310
	100.0%	100.0%	100.0%

Note: Many respondents did not know the birthplace of both parents or all grandparents. In these cases, we assigned both parents or grandparents the birthplace of the one whose birthplace was known.

TABLE 3.8 Household Size, by National Origin

Number in Household	Mexican	Puerto Rican	Cuban	Anglo
One	47	56	24	64
	5.3%	9.6%	7.7%	14.5%
Two	154	110	86	180
	17.6%	18.9%	27.6%	40.3%
Three	182	123	88	80
	20.8%	21.1%	28.2%	18.1%
Four	215	111	61	54
	24.5%	19.1%	19.5%	12.1%
Five or more	279	183	53	67
	31.8%	31.3%	16.9%	15.0%
Total	877	583	312	446
	100.0%	100.0%	100.0%	100.0%

TABLE 3.9 Tenancy, by National Origin

Tenancy	Mexican	Puerto Rican	Cuban	Anglo
Rent	307	414	104	120
	35.1%	70.6%	33.5%	28.5%
Live with parents, who own	61	29	29	0
	7.0%	5.0%	9.3%	0.0%
Own	431	78	151	269
	49.2%	13.3%	48.4%	63.8%
Other living arrangements	76	65	27	33
	8.7%	11.1%	8.7%	7.8%
Total	876	587	312	422
	100.0%	100.0%	100.0%	100.0%

C. Education, Income, and Employment (Tables 3.10–3.17)

Findings

Mexican and Puerto Rican respondents had lower levels of formal education than did either Cubans or Anglos (Table 3.10). Thirty percent of Puerto Ricans and approximately 20 percent of our Mexican and Cuban respondents attended school for eight or fewer years (compared to just 1 percent of Anglos). Almost one-third of Cuban respondents, however, had education beyond the high school level, compared to 10 percent of Mexicans and 20 percent of Anglos.

Puerto Rican households were the most likely to have no members working for pay (Table 3.11). Mexican and Cuban households had higher average numbers of household workers than did either Puerto Rican or Anglo households.

At both the household level and the individual level, Cuban and Anglo households earned more than Mexican or Puerto Rican households (Tables 3.12 and 3.13). This difference is particularly clear at the individual level. Cubans were nearly twice as likely as Mexicans and four times as likely as Puerto Ricans to have the highest per capita incomes (twenty thousand dollars per year or more). At the other extreme, just 5 percent of Cubans had per capita incomes of twenty-five hundred dollars per year or less compared with 27 percent for Puerto Ricans and 16 percent for Mexicans.

Cuban respondents had the highest labor force participation rates (Table 3.14). Puerto Ricans were the most likely to be either temporarily unemployed or completely out of the labor force.

Cubans were more likely to be found in higher-status occupations than were Anglos, Mexicans, or Puerto Ricans (Table 3.15).

Among those not in the work force, Cuban respondents were likely to be retired while Puerto Rican respondents were likely to be full-time homemakers (Table 3.16). Mexicans not in the labor force were relatively evenly divided between the retired and full-time homemakers.

Cuban respondents had a broader range of work-related experiences than did either Mexicans or Puerto Ricans (Table 3.17). The most common job skills for all national-origin groups were supervision and telephoning unknown individuals on business.

Questions Asked

12, 13, 14, 24, 25b, 26a, 26b, 27, 103a, 103b, 103c, 103d, 103e, 181, and 182.

TABLE 3.10 Education, by National Origin

Education	Mexican	Puerto Rican	Cuban	Anglo
0–8 years	177	175	60	5
	20.2%	30.0%	19.5%	1.1%
9–12 years, no degree	203	128	33	106
	23.2%	21.9%	10.7%	23.8%
High school diploma or GED	411	215	115	243
	46.9%	36.9%	37.2%	54.9%
Beyond high school	84	65	101	90
	9.6%	11.1%	32.6%	20.2%
Total	875	583	308	443
	100.0%	100.0%	100.0%	100.0%

TABLE 3.11 Household Wage Earners, by National Origin

Salaried Workers	Mexican	Puerto Rican	Cuban	Anglo
None	87	143	43	80
	9.9%	24.3%	13.7%	17.9%
One	240	202	71	145
	27.3%	34.5%	22.8%	32.6%
Two	356	164	126	166
	40.6%	27.9%	40.3%	37.2%
Three	140	59	57	38
	15.9%	10.0%	18.2%	8.6%
Four	43	13	11	9
	4.9%	2.2%	3.5%	2.1%
Five or more	12	6	4	7
	1.4%	1.1%	1.4%	1.6%
Total	878	587	312	446
	100.0%	100.0%	100.0%	100.0%

TABLE 3.12 Household Income, by National Origin

Household Income	Mexican	Puerto Rican	Cuban	Anglo
$0–$12,999	211	246	59	88
	25.5%	45.5%	19.7%	21.0%
$13,000–$19,999	138	91	41	50
	16.6%	16.8%	13.8%	11.9%
$20,000–$29,999	156	94	59	100
	18.8%	17.4%	19.7%	24.0%
$30,000–$39,999	151	62	47	66
	18.3%	11.5%	15.7%	15.9%
$40,000–$49,999	80	23	17	40
	9.7%	4.2%	5.5%	9.5%
$50,000+	91	25	76	74
	11.0%	4.6%	25.6%	17.7%
Total	828	541	298	418
	100.0%	100.0%	100.0%	100.0%

TABLE 3.13 Per Capita Household Income, by National Origin

Per Capita Annual Household Income	Mexican	Puerto Rican	Cuban	Anglo
$2,500 or less	140	155	14	20
	16.2%	26.9%	4.6%	4.7%
$2,501–$5,000	170	118	49	59
	19.7%	20.5%	15.7%	14.2%
$5,001–$10,000	283	175	96	110
	32.8%	30.2%	30.8%	26.3%
$10,001–$20,000	178	74	103	152
	20.5%	12.7%	32.9%	36.3%
$20,001+	57	15	36	77
	6.6%	2.7%	11.6%	18.5%
Refused to answer	37	41	14	0
	4.3%	7.1%	4.4%	0.0%
Total	865	578	312	418
	100.0%	100.0%	100.0%	100.0%

TABLE 3.14 Labor Force Status, by National Origin

Present Work Situation of Respondent	Mexican	Puerto Rican	Cuban	Anglo
In labor force	528	293	214	283
	60.2%	50.0%	68.6%	63.8%
Temporarily unemployed	104	71	19	23
	11.9%	12.1%	6.2%	5.2%
Not in labor force	244	222	79	137
	27.9%	37.9%	25.2%	31.0%
Total	876	586	312	443
	100.0%	100.0%	100.0%	100.0%

TABLE 3.15 Occupation, by National Origin

Occupation	Mexican	Puerto Rican	Cuban	Anglo
Managerial, professional, or specialty	83	37	56	65
	9.6%	6.4%	17.9%	14.8%
Technical, sales, or administrative support	177	98	101	90
	20.3%	16.9%	32.5%	20.6%
Service	103	72	16	38
	11.8%	12.4%	5.0%	8.7%
Farming, forestry, or fishing	16	4	2	5
	1.9%	0.7%	0.6%	1.1%
Precision production or crafts	85	32	16	48
	9.7%	5.6%	5.0%	11.0%
Operator, fabricator, or laborer	131	90	38	39
	15.0%	15.4%	12.2%	9.0%
Not in labor force	276	249	83	152
	31.7%	42.7%	26.8%	34.7%
Total	871	583	311	437
	100.0%	100.0%	100.0%	100.0%

TABLE 3.16 Reason for Not Being in the Work Force, by National Origin

Reason for Not Being in the Labor Force	*Mexican*	*Puerto Rican*	*Cuban*	*Anglo*
Unemployed	35	29	5	17
	12.8%	11.8%	5.8%	11.3%
Disabled	17	33	4	5
	6.2%	13.1%	4.7%	3.1%
Retired	93	49	48	95
	33.8%	19.8%	58.1%	62.4%
Homemaker	104	116	22	28
	37.5%	46.4%	26.8%	18.4%
Student	27	22	4	7
	9.8%	8.8%	4.6%	4.8%
Total	276	249	83	152
	100.0%	100.0%	100.0%	100.0%

TABLE 3.17 Work-Related Experiences, by National Origin

Experience	*Mexican*	*Puerto Rican*	*Cuban*	*Anglo*
Supervise others at job	226	127	78	143
	44.8%	33.5%	48.3%	48.1%
	(n=504)	(n=379)	(n=161)	(n=297)
Write a letter on the job	141	78	109	109
	24.0%	24.6%	48.2%	37.8%
	(n=587)	(n=315)	(n=226)	(n=289)
Telephone an unknown person as part of job	255	130	124	194
	43.5%	41.1%	55.2%	67.2%
	(n=587)	(n=315)	(n=225)	(n=289)
Attend business meeting	248	129	114	194
	42.3%	41.0%	50.6%	67.0%
	(n=587)	(n=315)	(n=225)	(n=289)
Give a presentation at a meeting	116	84	60	95
	19.7%	26.8%	26.5%	32.9%
	(n=587)	(n=315)	(n=225)	(n=289)
Talk to government official	85	35	41	50
	14.5%	11.2%	18.4%	17.4%
	(n=586)	(n=315)	(n=225)	(n=289)

D. Religion (Tables 3.18–3.21)

Findings

The majority of Latino respondents were Catholic (Table 3.18). Anglos were more likely to be Protestant.

Approximately one-third of Puerto Ricans and Anglos had had born-again experiences (Table 3.19). Fewer than 30 percent of Mexicans and fewer than 20 percent of Cubans had had these experiences.

Latinos were more likely than Anglos to report that religion provided quite a bit of guidance in their lives (Table 3.20). Mexican respondents reported the highest levels of guidance from religion.

Cuban and Mexican respondents were the most likely to attend religious services at least once a month (Table 3.21). More than 45 percent of the respondents from each of the Latino national-origin groups and more than 50 percent of Anglo respondents never or almost never attended religious services.

Questions Asked

20a, 20b, 21, 22, and 23.

TABLE 3.18 Religious Affiliation, by National Origin

Religious Affiliation	Mexican	Puerto Rican	Cuban	Anglo
Catholic	645	382	233	95
	73.7%	65.1%	74.8%	21.2%
Protestant	132	131	45	242
	15.0%	22.3%	14.4%	54.2%
Other/no preference	98	73	34	109
	11.3%	12.5%	10.9%	24.5%
Total	875	587	312	446
	100.0%	100.0%	100.0%	100.0%

TABLE 3.19 Born-Again Religious Experience, by National Origin

Born-Again Religious Experience	Mexican	Puerto Rican	Cuban	Anglo
No	576	346	230	244
	71.0%	64.3%	80.6%	66.9%
Yes	235	192	55	121
	29.0%	35.7%	19.4%	33.1%
Total	811	538	286	365
	100.0%	100.0%	100.0%	100.0%

TABLE 3.20 Religious Guidance, by National Origin

Guidance Received from Religion	Mexican	Puerto Rican	Cuban	Anglo
None	45	35	15	25
	5.6%	6.4%	5.3%	6.8%
Some	258	176	92	142
	31.8%	32.5%	32.1%	38.7%
Quite a bit	255	172	97	80
	31.4%	31.9%	34.1%	21.7%
A great deal	253	157	82	121
	31.2%	29.1%	28.5%	32.9%
Total	811	540	286	368
	100.0%	100.0%	100.0%	100.0%

TABLE 3.21 Attendance at Religious Services, by National Origin

Attendance at Religious Services	Mexican	Puerto Rican	Cuban	Anglo
Never	411	227	129	203
	46.8%	38.7%	41.3%	46.0%
Almost never	26	45	17	29
	3.0%	7.7%	5.4%	6.6%
A few times a year	76	93	34	75
	8.7%	15.9%	10.9%	17.1%
Once/twice a month	201	119	82	92
	22.9%	20.2%	26.3%	20.8%
Almost every week	164	102	50	42
	18.7%	17.4%	16.0%	9.5%
Total	877	587	312	441
	100.0%	100.0%	100.0%	100.0%

4

Psychological, Cultural, Linguistic, and Associational Characteristics of U.S. Citizens

This chapter examines four aspects of the respondents' lives that are particularly important in explaining the development and maintenance of their political and social attitudes and behaviors: (1) psychological orientations; (2) cultural characteristics; (3) linguistic patterns; and (4) social networks and social distance.

One factor deserves special note. Among the most unexpected and important findings of the LNPS is the degree to which Mexican and Puerto Rican respondents were either bilingual or English-dominant. A majority of respondents from each of these groups used English or a mixture of English and Spanish at home. Cuban respondents were more likely to use Spanish at home. In all three national-origin groups, the majority rated themselves bilingual or better in English. Just 12 percent of citizen respondents who traced their ancestry to Mexico rated themselves as better in Spanish than in English.

These findings should counter the frequently heard assertions that Latinos are unwilling to learn English and are fighting to maintain Spanish. Instead, they show that Spanish exclusivity would make communication difficult for 61 percent of Mexican-origin U.S. citizens, 34 percent of Puerto Ricans, and 29 percent of Cuban-origin U.S. citizens.

A. Psychological Orientations (Tables 4.1–4.5)

Findings

Although the Mexican, Puerto Rican, and Cuban respondents expressed more caution about how much they could trust others (Table 4.1) and how helpful people were (Table 4.2) than did Anglos, the majority of each group expressed belief in the traditionally American values of hard work and support for equal opportunity (Table 4.3). Bare majorities of each national-origin group accepted inequality of chance.

Regardless of national origin, approximately 45 percent of respondents believed that their financial status had improved in the twelve months prior to being interviewed, 1988-1989 (Table 4.4). Between 9 percent (among Cubans) and 16 percent (among Mexicans) felt that their economic condition had deteriorated.

Between 60 percent and 65 percent of respondents anticipated that in the year following their LNPS interview their financial condition would improve (Table 4.5). Six percent or less of each national-origin group was pessimistic about their short-term economic futures.

Questions Asked

139, 140, 141a, 141b, 152, 153, 156a, and 156b.

TABLE 4.1   Trust of Others, by National Origin

Degree of Trust	Mexican	Puerto Rican	Cuban	Anglo
Trust most people	139	35	44	165
	15.9%	5.9%	14.0%	37.0%
Must be careful with most people	734	552	268	280
	84.1%	94.1%	86.0%	63.0%
Total	873	586	312	445
	100.0%	100.0%	100.0%	100.0%

TABLE 4.2   Belief in Helpfulness of People, by National Origin

Degree of Helpfulness	Mexican	Puerto Rican	Cuban	Anglo
People try to help each other	376	142	90	236
	43.1%	24.6%	29.2%	53.5%
Others look out for themselves	497	437	218	205
	56.9%	75.4%	70.8%	46.5%
Total	872	580	308	441
	100.0%	100.0%	100.0%	100.0%

TABLE 4.3 Who or What Determines Success and Opportunity, by National Origin

Belief	Mexican	Puerto Rican	Cuban
Success determined by outsiders	396	271	120
	47.4%	49.1%	40.8%
	(n=838)	(n=551)	(n=293)
Hard work leads to success	503	305	183
	58.2%	54.9%	61.6%
	(n=862)	(n=554)	(n=297)
Society should promote equal opportunity	827	557	295
	96.0%	96.9%	98.3%
	(n=862)	(n=575)	(n=300)
Inequality by chance is acceptable	435	294	155
	52.0%	54.1%	51.3%
	(n=837)	(n=544)	(n=303)

TABLE 4.4 Self-Evaluation of Financial Status, by National Origin

Family's Financial Status Now Compared to Twelve Months Before Survey	Mexican	Puerto Rican	Cuban
Much better off	80	53	35
	9.1%	9.0%	11.1%
Better off	313	228	110
	35.6%	38.9%	35.2%
The same	342	227	140
	39.0%	38.7%	45.1%
Worse off	122	68	26
	13.9%	11.7%	8.2%
Much worse off	22	10	1
	2.5%	1.7%	0.4%
Total	878	587	312
	100.0%	100.0%	100.0%

TABLE 4.5   Self-Evaluation of Anticipated Financial Status, by National Origin

Anticipated Family Financial Condition Twelve Months After Survey	*Mexican*	*Puerto Rican*	*Cuban*
Much better off	162	102	51
	18.5%	17.7%	16.5%
Better off	371	273	134
	42.4%	47.4%	43.4%
The same	296	175	115
	33.8%	30.4%	37.2%
Worse off	43	24	9
	5.0%	4.2%	2.9%
Much worse off	3	2	0
	0.3%	0.3%	0.0%
Total	875	576	309
	100.0%	100.0%	100.0%

B. Cultural Characteristics (Tables 4.6 and 4.7)

Findings

The preferred identification of most respondents was a national-origin-based term (Table 4.6). Approximately three-quarters of Puerto Ricans and two-thirds of Cubans and Mexicans preferred a national-origin-based identification term. The national-origin terms for Mexicans are Mexican, Mexicano(a), Mexican American, Chicano(a), and Raza. For Puerto Ricans, they are Puerto Rican and Niuyorican/Neorican. Cuban is the only identification term offered to Cubans in the survey. Pan-ethnic identification terms are more popular for all national-origin groups than an identification as American. Pan-ethnic identification terms include Hispanic, Latino, Spanish, Spanish American, and Hispano. While Mexicans were three times as likely to prefer a pan-ethnic term to American, Cubans were only slightly more likely to prefer the ethnic identification.

Among the minority of respondents who had opinions about the meanings of the terms "Latino" and "Hispanic," the majority defined these identities in pan-ethnic terms—an identity broader than one's own national origin—such as "people from Latin America or Spain," "born and reared in a Spanish-speaking country," or "a mixture of races" (Table 4.7).

Questions Asked

4, 5, 6, and 7.

TABLE 4.6   Preferred Ethnic Identification, by National Origin

Ethnic Identification	Mexican	Puerto Rican	Cuban
Mexican origin	544	5	0
	63.3%	0.9%	0.0%
Puerto Rican origin	2	437	4
	0.3%	74.9%	1.2%
Cuban origin	0	0	192
	0.0%	0.1%	64.0%
Pan-ethnic	239	88	54
	27.8%	15.0%	18.1%
American	73	53	50
	8.5%	9.1%	16.7%
Total	859	584	300
	100.0%	100.0%	100.0%

Notes: The preferred identification terms among Mexican respondents are Mexican (117), Mexicano(a) (79), Mexican American (316), Chicano(a) (31), Puerto Rican (2), Hispanic (143), Latino(a) (13), Spanish (27), Spanish American (47), Raza (1), Hispano (9), and American (73).

Puerto Rican respondents prefer the following identity terms: Mexican (5), Puerto Rican (428), Niuyorican (9), Hispanic (20), Latino(a) (7), Spanish (8), Spanish American (42), Hispano (10), and American (53).

Among Cuban respondents, the preferred terms are Cuban (192), Puerto Rican (4), Hispanic (16), Latino(a) (7), Spanish (4), Spanish American (23), Hispano (5), and American (50).

TABLE 4.7 Meaning of Terms "Latino" and "Hispanic," by National Origin

Meaning of Terms "Latino" and Hispanic	Mexican	Puerto Rican	Cuban
Pan-ethnic	336	294	128
	87.1%	129.3%	150.3%
National origin-specific	154	59	12
	39.9%	25.9%	13.8%
Other, or has no meaning	44	18	6
	11.5%	7.9%	6.7%
No opinion	492	360	227
	56.0%	61.3%	72.8%
Total	878	587	312
	100.0%	100.0%	100.0%

Note: Respondents could provide up to two definitions of Latino and two definitions of Hispanic. Therefore, the number of meanings is greater than the number of respondents.

C. Linguistic Patterns (Tables 4.8–4.11)

Findings

When evaluating the following data, it is important to note that 13 percent of the Mexican, 66 percent of the Puerto Rican, and 71 percent of the Cuban respondents were foreign-born, that is, born in a Spanish-speaking nation.

No more than 10 percent of these U.S. citizen respondents from any of the national-origin groups were monolingual in either Spanish or English (Table 4.8). The majority of U.S. citizen respondents were either bilingual or English-dominant. Cuban respondents were most likely to rate their Spanish better than their English (43 percent); Mexican respondents were most likely to rate their English better than their Spanish (62 percent).

Although Spanish dominance or exclusivity was somewhat more common for home language use, the pattern follows the general patterns of overall language ability (Table 4.9). At home, 15 percent of Mexican U.S. citizen families used Spanish more than English. More than 60 percent of Cubans, on the other hand, spoke Spanish more than English. Puerto Rican language use patterns fell between these two extremes. Approximately 44 percent of Puerto Rican households used Spanish more than English and 25 percent used English more than Spanish.

The language used by the respondent to answer the survey is a good indicator of the absence of literacy in the language not used (Tables 4.10 and 4.11). As determined by a test used in the LNPS, the majority of Spanish-speaking interviewees had low English-language literacy and the majority of English-speaking interviewees had low Spanish literacy. This disparity was most marked among Cuban respondents.

Questions Asked

168, 169, and SAQ2.

TABLE 4.8 Overall Language Ability, by National Origin

Overall Language Ability	Mexican	Puerto Rican	Cuban
Only Spanish	6	43	17
	0.6%	7.3%	5.3%
Better in Spanish	98	198	118
	11.1%	33.7%	37.7%
No difference	227	146	88
	25.9%	24.9%	28.2%
Better in English	482	183	83
	54.9%	31.2%	26.6%
Only English	65	16	7
	7.4%	2.8%	2.2%
Total	877	587	312
	100.0%	100.0%	100.0%

TABLE 4.9 Home Language of Respondent, by National Origin

Language Spoken in the Home	Mexican	Puerto Rican	Cuban
Only Spanish	46	124	117
	5.3%	21.1%	37.7%
More Spanish than English	84	136	73
	9.6%	23.2%	23.3%
Both languages	234	175	78
	26.7%	29.9%	25.0%
More English than Spanish	275	90	27
	31.3%	15.3%	8.6%
Only English	238	61	17
	27.1%	10.5%	5.5%
Total	878	586	312
	100.0%	100.0%	100.0%

TABLE 4.10   English Literacy of Respondents Interviewed in Spanish, by National Origin

English Literacy of the Spanish-Dominant	Mexican	Puerto Rican	Cuban
Low	99	160	129
	62.5%	52.0%	66.5%
High	60	148	65
	37.5%	48.0%	33.5%
Total	159	308	195
	100.0%	100.0%	100.0%

TABLE 4.11   Spanish Literacy of Respondents Interviewed in English, by National Origin

Spanish Literacy of the English-Dominant	Mexican	Puerto Rican	Cuban
Low	380	183	90
	52.9%	65.7%	79.3%
High	339	95	23
	47.1%	34.3%	20.7%
Total	719	278	113
	100.0%	100.0%	100.0%

D. Social Networks and Social Distance (Tables 4.12–4.16)

Findings

Cubans were slightly more likely to associate with fellow Cubans than Mexicans or Puerto Ricans were with their co-ethnics (Table 4.12). More than 85 percent of each national-origin group found at least as many co-ethnics as non-co-ethnics in organizations to which they belonged. It is important to note that many fewer respondents belonged to organizations than participated in the other three activities mentioned.

Cubans, Mexicans, and Puerto Ricans did not report a great deal of inter-national-origin-group association (Tables 4.13–4.15). Among the three groups, the pairing that had the highest contact was Cubans and Puerto Ricans.

The low levels of intergroup contact may explain the low reported closeness between the groups (Table 4.16). The median response on a scale of 0 to 100 is most often the midpoint of 50. Only Puerto Rican feelings toward Mexican Americans (60) and Cubans feelings toward

Puerto Ricans in the United States (75) exceeded 50. Each group felt closer to Anglos than it did to any of the other Latino national-origin groups.

Each group thought highly of itself. Mexicans and Puerto Ricans each rated their feelings toward their own group at 100. The median Cuban feeling toward other Cubans was 95.

Questions Asked

60, 170, 171, 172, 177, 178, 179, and SAQ1.

TABLE 4.12 Ethnicity of Social Contacts, by National Origin

Half or More Co-Ethnic	Mexican	Puerto Rican	Cuban
At social occasions	688	473	269
	79.8%	86.6%	90.6%
	(n=862)	(n=546)	(n=297)
Among friends	721	497	281
	82.5%	86.3%	90.4%
	(n=874)	(n=576)	(n=311)
Where respondent relaxes	637	460	250
	74.9%	82.0%	83.6%
	(n=851)	(n=561)	(n=299)
In organizations to which respondent belongs	311	141	110
	92.8%	86.5%	93.2%
	(n=336)	(n=163)	(n=118)

TABLE 4.13 Contact With Mexicans, by National Origin

Contacts With Mexican-Origin Individuals	Mexican	Puerto Rican	Cuban
A lot	460	80	11
	52.4%	13.8%	4.0%
Some	266	110	28
	30.3%	19.1%	10.2%
Little	128	158	87
	14.6%	27.5%	31.4%
None	24	228	151
	2.8%	39.6%	54.4%
Total	878	575	278
	100.0%	100.0%	100.0%

TABLE 4.14 Contact With Puerto Ricans, by National Origin

Contact With Puerto Rican–Origin Individuals	Mexican	Puerto Rican	Cuban
A lot	20	395	42
	2.3%	67.4%	15.1%
Some	75	104	99
	8.6%	17.7%	35.8%
Little	187	69	73
	21.3%	11.8%	26.3%
None	593	18	63
	67.8%	4.1%	22.9%
Total	875	587	277
	100.0%	100.0%	100.0%

TABLE 4.15 Contact With Cubans, by National Origin

Contact With Cuban-Origin Individuals	Mexican	Puerto Rican	Cuban
A lot	10	58	251
	1.1%	10.0%	80.4%
Some	41	101	31
	4.7%	17.5%	10.0%
Little	147	180	25
	16.8%	31.3%	8.1%
None	677	237	5
	77.4%	41.1%	1.5%
Total	875	575	312
	100.0%	100.0%	100.0%

TABLE 4.16 Closeness to Ethnic Groups, by National Origin (Median Score)

Closeness to	Mexican	Puerto Rican	Cuban	Anglo
Mexican Americans	100 (n=865)	60 (n=549)	50 (n=294)	65 (n=432)
Mexican immigrants	75 (n=857)	50 (n=548)	50 (n=293)	50 (n=427)
African Americans	60 (n=854)	60 (n=546)	50 (n=294)	60 (n=435)
Puerto Ricans in the U.S.	50 (n=805)	100 (n=570)	75 (n=298)	50 (n=404)
Puerto Ricans in Puerto Rico	50 (n=768)	100 (n=562)	75 (n=294)	50 (n=402)
Anglos	75 (n=859)	75 (n=549)	85 (n=296)	80 (n=431)
Cubans in the United States	50 (n=797)	50 (n=547)	95 (n=299)	50 (n=409)
Asians	50 (n=796)	50 (n=526)	55 (n=295)	50 (n=431)
Jews	50 (n=779)	50 (n=516)	60 (n=293)	70 (n=425)

5

Information Environment of U.S. Citizens

In this chapter, we examine the levels and types of information available to survey respondents. We examine three interrelated questions: (1) media use; (2) problem solving; and (3) political knowledge.

The patterns of information acquisition and use indicate that citizens, regardless of national origin, rely largely on television for news. Although few respondents overall discussed public policy concerns, those who did spoke equally with friends, family, and associates. Three measures of political knowledge suggest that respondents were somewhat informed about U.S. political actors and institutions. Mexican and Puerto Rican respondents were slightly less knowledgeable than were Cuban and Anglo respondents.

A. Media Use (Tables 5.1–5.4)

Findings

Television was the most frequently cited source of news (Table 5.1); newspapers were the second-most-frequently used news source. Anglos and Cubans relied on newspapers at higher rates than did Mexicans or Puerto Ricans.

English-language media were preferred to either bilingual or Spanish-language media (Table 5.2). More than three-quarters of Mexican citizen respondents used English media exclusively.

Most respondents read newspapers at least once during the week prior to being interviewed (Table 5.3); however, a substantial minority of Latino respondents read a newspaper four to seven days that week.

A majority of respondents looked to television for news four to seven days of the week prior to being interviewed (Table 5.4). Cuban and Puerto Rican respondents were more likely than Anglo or Mexican respondents to view television news frequently.

Questions Asked

48, 49, 50, 51, 52, and 53.

TABLE 5.1 Most-Used News Source, by National Origin

Most-Used News Source	Mexican	Puerto Rican	Cuban	Anglo
Television	654	456	218	283
	75.3%	78.9%	70.7%	64.5%
Newspapers	146	78	63	115
	16.8%	13.6%	20.5%	26.3%
Magazines	7	3	2	7
	0.8%	0.5%	0.5%	1.5%
Radio	62	41	25	34
	7.1%	7.1%	8.2%	7.7%
Total	869	578	309	439
	100.0%	100.0%	100.0%	100.0%

TABLE 5.2 Language of Two Most-Used News Sources, by National Origin

Language of News Sources	Mexican	Puerto Rican	Cuban
English	655	232	149
	76.8%	40.9%	49.5%
Both English and Spanish	156	206	82
	18.3%	36.2%	27.3%
Spanish	42	130	70
	4.9%	22.8%	23.2%
Total	853	568	301
	100.0%	100.0%	100.0%

TABLE 5.3 Newspaper Readership, by National Origin

Frequency of Newspaper Readership for Political News During the Week Preceding the LNPS Interview	*Mexican*	*Puerto Rican*	*Cuban*	*Anglo*
Don't read newspaper	9	8	3	7
	1.0%	1.4%	1.0%	1.6%
0 days	277	181	90	94
	31.7%	30.9%	28.9%	21.2%
1–3 days	285	196	69	115
	32.5%	33.4%	22.1%	25.9%
4–7 days	305	201	149	228
	34.9%	34.3%	48.0%	51.3%
Total	875	586	311	445
	100.0%	100.0%	100.0%	100.0%

TABLE 5.4 Television Viewership for News, by National Origin

Frequency of Watching Television News During Week Preceding LNPS Interview	*Mexican*	*Puerto Rican*	*Cuban*	*Anglo*
Don't watch television news	9	8	3	7
	1.0%	1.4%	1.0%	1.6%
0 days	104	49	21	42
	11.9%	8.4%	6.8%	9.5%
1–3 days	288	123	59	126
	32.9%	20.9%	19.1%	28.4%
4–7 days	474	406	227	268
	54.3%	69.3%	73.0%	60.6%
Total	874	585	311	443
	100.0%	100.0%	100.0%	100.0%

B. Problem Solving (Table 5.5)

Findings

For the most part, respondents did not talk about political issues (Table 5.5). However, among those who did, the people with whom they talked were most frequently friends and family. Cubans and Anglos were more likely to talk about political problems than were Mexicans and Puerto Ricans.

Questions Asked

113 and 114.

TABLE 5.5 People With Whom Respondent Discussed Political Problems, by National Origin

Persons With Whom Respondent Talked About Local or National Political Problems	Mexican	Puerto Rican	Cuban	Anglo
Family and friends	169	90	92	99
	19.3%	15.3%	29.6%	22.3%
Social and professional associates	89	50	43	76
	10.1%	8.5%	13.7%	17.1%
Public officials	14	9	2	10
	1.6%	1.5%	0.6%	2.2%
Other	7	12	3	6
	0.8%	2.1%	1.0%	1.4%
Did not talk about political problems	597	426	172	253
	68.1%	72.6%	55.0%	56.9%
Total	876	587	312	445
	100.0%	100.0%	100.0%	100.0%

C. Political Knowledge (Tables 5.6–5.10)

Findings

Most respondents followed current affairs some or most of the time (Table 5.6). Overall, Cuban respondents were most likely to follow current affairs "most of the time." Ten percent or fewer of respondents from the four national-origin groups followed current affairs "hardly at all."

Approximately 20 percent of each national-origin group knew public officials personally (Table 5.7).

A majority of respondents could correctly identify the ideological positions of Ronald Reagan and Jesse Jackson (Tables 5.8 and 5.9); however, approximately 32 percent of Mexican respondents, 31 percent of Puerto Rican respondents, 15 percent of Anglo respondents, and 12 percent of Cuban respondents placed Ronald Reagan on the liberal side of the political spectrum. Twenty percent of Puerto Ricans, 19 percent of Mexicans, 10 percent of Cubans, and 8 percent of Anglos placed Jesse Jackson on the Right.

Few who tried to identify Dan Quayle answered incorrectly (Table 5.10). Approximately one-third of Mexican and one-sixth of Cuban respondents did not attempt to answer the question. Fewer people tried to identify William Rehnquist. Of those who tried, more than half were partially or fully incorrect, regardless of national origin.

More respondents tried to and succeeded in identifying the party with the majority of members in Congress. Of those who tried to answer the question, 20 percent of the Cubans, 30 percent of the Anglos and the Puerto Ricans, and 40 percent of the Mexicans answered incorrectly.

Questions Asked

54, 104, 131a, 131b, 132, 143, 144.

TABLE 5.6 Attentiveness to Current Affairs, by National Origin

Follows Current Affairs	Mexican	Puerto Rican	Cuban	Anglo
Most of the time	275	199	142	196
	31.8%	34.6%	46.2%	44.8%
Some of the time	296	182	103	154
	34.2%	31.5%	33.4%	35.1%
Now and then	208	159	41	72
	24.0%	27.6%	13.3%	16.5%
Hardly at all	87	37	22	16
	10.0%	6.4%	7.1%	3.6%
Total	866	577	308	438
	100.0%	100.0%	100.0%	100.0%

TABLE 5.7 Acquaintance with a Public Official, by National Origin

Acquaintance with a Public Official	Mexican	Puerto Rican	Cuban	Anglo
Yes	165	125	62	87
	18.9%	21.3%	20.0%	19.6%
No	711	461	249	358
	81.1%	78.7%	80.0%	80.4%
Total	876	586	312	446
	100.0%	100.0%	100.0%	100.0%

TABLE 5.8 Ideological Categorization of Ronald Reagan, by National Origin

Ronald Reagan's Ideology	Mexican	Puerto Rican	Cuban	Anglo
Very liberal	108	48	8	26
	12.8%	8.8%	2.5%	6.0%
Liberal	105	75	20	29
	12.4%	13.7%	6.6%	6.7%
Slightly liberal	61	47	10	14
	7.2%	8.6%	3.3%	3.4%
Moderate	112	94	37	62
	13.3%	17.1%	12.2%	14.6%
Slightly conservative	72	48	22	60
	8.5%	8.7%	7.1%	14.1%
Conservative	215	139	130	125
	25.4%	25.4%	42.8%	29.3%
Very conservative	172	98	78	111
	20.4%	17.8%	25.5%	25.9%
Total	845	548	305	428
	100.0%	100.0%	100.0%	100.0%

TABLE 5.9 Ideological Categorization of Jesse Jackson, by National Origin

Jesse Jackson's Ideology	Mexican	Puerto Rican	Cuban	Anglo
Very liberal	156	92	108	105
	19.0%	17.1%	37.3%	24.9%
Liberal	290	141	100	178
	35.3%	26.3%	34.5%	42.3%
Slightly liberal	88	85	31	49
	10.7%	15.9%	10.6%	11.7%
Moderate	134	114	21	54
	16.4%	21.2%	7.2%	12.9%
Slightly conservative	44	39	13	14
	5.3%	7.3%	4.5%	3.4%
Conservative	70	49	14	16
	8.5%	9.1%	4.7%	3.7%
Very conservative	39	17	4	5
	4.8%	3.1%	1.2%	1.1%
Total	821	535	289	420
	100.0%	100.0%	100.0%	100.0%

TABLE 5.10 Political Knowledge, by National Origin

Correctly Identified	Mexican	Puerto Rican	Cuban	Anglo
Dan Quayle	550	286	247	391
	93.5%	94.5%	98.4%	98.4%
	(n=588)	(n=303)	(n=251)	(n=397)
William Rehnquist	32	16	25	79
	27.9%	27.4%	38.0%	46.7%
	(n=115)	(n=57)	(n=66)	(n=170)
Party with most members in House	414	292	223	274
	58.5%	66.6%	79.2%	70.2%
	(n=708)	(n=438)	(n=282)	(n=390)

6

Political Values of U.S. Citizens

This chapter describes three aspects of political values among Mexicans, Puerto Ricans, Cubans, and Anglos: (1) feelings about the U.S. government; (2) political tolerance; and (3) ideology and perception of the government's role in solving public policy problems.

The answers to the questions concerning political values are important for both the citizen and the polity because they indicate the linkage between the government and the individual. Overall, the results of the Latino National Political Survey suggest that Latinos have a strong attachment to the United States. Despite a self-professed moderate conservatism, they also express a series of demands for increased government role in creating and shaping public policies to meet their needs.

A. Feelings About the U.S. Government (Tables 6.1–6.4)

Findings

The great majority of respondents, regardless of national origin, expressed "very" or "extremely" strong love for and levels of pride in the United States (Tables 6.1 and 6.2). Cubans and Anglos expressed the strongest attachments.

Only among some of the Puerto Rican respondents was this attachment tempered, with 23 percent expressing "somewhat" strong love and 8 percent expressing "not very strong" love. Levels of pride were also somewhat lower among Puerto Rican respondents.

Overall, respondents expressed less trust for the government than they felt love for or pride in the United States (Table 6.3). Cuban respondents were most likely always to trust government officials to do what is right (18.3 percent). Anglo respondents were least likely always to trust the government (1.4 percent).

Despite these general feelings of support for the U.S. government, the majority of Anglos, Mexicans, and Puerto Ricans felt that government was run by the few in their own interests (Table 6.4). Almost two-thirds of Cubans, on the other hand, believed that government was run for the benefit of all.

Questions Asked

46, 47, 107, and 108

TABLE 6.1 Love for the United States, by National Origin

Strength of Love for U.S.	Mexican	Puerto Rican	Cuban	Anglo
Extremely strong	343	185	178	220
	39.1%	31.5%	57.2%	49.4%
Very strong	392	218	96	190
	44.7%	37.1%	30.7%	42.8%
Somewhat strong	124	136	35	30
	14.1%	23.2%	11.3%	6.7%
Not very strong	18	47	2	5
	2.1%	8.1%	0.8%	1.1%
Total	878	586	312	446
	100.0%	100.0%	100.0%	100.0%

TABLE 6.2 Pride in United States, by National Origin

Degree of Pride in United States	Mexican	Puerto Rican	Cuban	Anglo
Extremely proud	386	222	162	270
	44.3%	38.5%	53.2%	61.0%
Very proud	405	256	116	136
	46.5%	44.6%	38.1%	30.8%
Somewhat proud	68	85	23	32
	7.8%	14.7%	7.5%	7.3%
Not very proud	13	13	3	4
	1.5%	2.3%	1.1%	0.9%
Total	871	576	305	442
	100.0%	100.0%	100.0%	100.0%

TABLE 6.3 Trust, by National Origin

Degree of Trust in Government Officials to Do What Is Right	Mexican	Puerto Rican	Cuban	Anglo
Just about always	65	75	57	6
	7.5%	12.8%	18.3%	1.4%
Most of the time	286	165	94	150
	32.7%	28.3%	30.3%	33.7%
Some of the time	424	265	137	246
	48.5%	45.4%	44.3%	55.3%
Almost never	99	78	22	43
	11.3%	13.5%	7.1%	9.6%
Total	875	582	309	444
	100.0%	100.0%	100.0%	100.0%

TABLE 6.4 Who Government Serves, by National Origin

Government is Run	Mexican	Puerto Rican	Cuban	Anglo
By the few in their interest	429	282	108	228
	51.3%	51.0%	35.9%	57.1%
For benefit of all	407	271	192	171
	48.7%	49.0%	64.1%	42.9%
Total	836	553	300	398
	100.0%	100.0%	100.0%	100.0%

B. Political Tolerance (Tables 6.5 and 6.6)

Findings

Among Mexican, Puerto Rican, and Anglo respondents, the most-disliked group in society was the Ku Klux Klan (Table 6.5). Cuban respondents most disliked Communists, the second-most-disliked group for Mexicans and Puerto Ricans.

Respondents expressed little tolerance for members of the disliked group holding public office, teaching in schools, or holding rallies (Table 6.6). Though also intolerant, Anglos were less intolerant than any of the Latino national-origin groups in allowing members of the disliked group to hold a rally.

Questions Asked

145, 146a, 146b, and 146c.

TABLE 6.5   Most-Disliked Group, by National Origin

Most-Disliked Group	Mexican	Puerto Rican	Cuban	Anglo
Communists	156	132	151	68
	18.0%	22.7%	48.8%	15.5%
Nazis	144	58	40	133
	16.5%	10.0%	12.9%	30.4%
Ku Klux Klan	338	216	78	149
	38.8%	37.2%	25.2%	34.1%
Homosexuals	134	125	22	36
	15.4%	21.5%	7.2%	8.2%
Black Muslims	14	7	2	11
	1.6%	1.2%	0.5%	2.5%
U.S. English	20	19	4	0
	2.3%	3.2%	1.4%	0.0%
Atheists	47	22	8	30
	5.4%	3.8%	2.7%	6.9%
Other	17	2	4	10
	1.9%	0.3%	1.3%	2.3%
Total	870	580	310	436
	100.0%	100.0%	100.0%	100.0%

TABLE 6.6   Tolerance of Disliked Groups, by National Origin

Member of Disliked Group	Mexican	Puerto Rican	Cuban	Anglo
May hold office	153	94	56	79
	17.8%	16.5%	18.6%	18.5%
	(n=859)	(n=567)	(n=305)	(n=427)
May teach	95	69	23	69
	11.2%	12.3%	7.4%	15.9%
	(n=854)	(n=569)	(n=310)	(n=431)
May hold rally	138	102	63	139
	16.2%	18.1%	20.8%	32.4%
	(n=852)	(n=562)	(n=306)	(n=429)

C. Ideology and Government Role in Solving Public Policy Problems
(Tables 6.7–6.11)

Findings

The self-professed ideology of the majority of respondents, regardless of national origin, was moderate to conservative (Table 6.7). Just 29 percent of Mexicans and Puerto Ricans, 26 percent of Anglos, and 23 percent of Cubans rated themselves as slightly liberal, liberal, or very liberal. Respondents evaluating themselves as slightly to very conservative numbered 36 percent for the Mexicans, 39 percent for the Anglos, 47 percent for the Puerto Ricans, and 55 percent for the Cubans.

Despite this alleged conservatism, more than nine in ten of the Latinos and almost as many Anglos believed that the government needs to get involved in solving national problems (Table 6.8). By extremely large majorities, all groups, particularly Puerto Ricans and Cubans, saw government as the solution to local problems. Cubans and Puerto Ricans saw a larger government role in solving local problems than in solving national problems.

On a series of specific policy issues—jobs, housing, and minimum income—respondents varied in their perceptions of whether government or individuals must develop the solutions (Tables 6.9 to 6.11). Only Puerto Ricans of the four national-origin groups were more likely to believe that government should provide jobs (we combined the first and second responses to develop a "government" score and the fourth and fifth to develop an "individual" score). Housing, on the other hand, saw a plurality of the three Latino national-origin groups in favor of government provision while Anglos were divided on the issue. All four groups were more likely to place the responsibility for providing a minimum income with the individual.

Questions Asked

110, 112, 128, 129, 130, and 142.

TABLE 6.7 Ideology, by National Origin

Ideology	Mexican	Puerto Rican	Cuban	Anglo
Very liberal	42 4.9%	40 7.0%	11 3.6%	16 3.7%
Liberal	100 11.6%	71 12.3%	40 13.0%	40 9.1%
Slightly liberal	104 12.1%	53 9.2%	19 6.3%	58 13.3%
Moderate	305 35.4%	142 24.7%	69 22.5%	152 34.6%
Slightly conservative	128 14.8%	93 16.3%	44 14.3%	72 16.3%
Conservative	133 15.4%	130 22.7%	106 34.2%	78 17.8%
Very conservative	50 5.8%	45 7.8%	18 6.0%	23 · 5.2%
Total	863 100.0%	574 100.0%	308 100.0%	439 100.0%

TABLE 6.8 Who Is Responsible for Solving National and Local Problems, by National Origin

Who Should Solve Problems?	Mexican	Puerto Rican	Cuban	Anglo
National problems				
Government	759 92.0%	517 91.9%	291 95.3%	370 85.6%
Individual	66 8.0%	46 8.1%	14 4.7%	62 14.4%
Total	824 100.0%	563 100.0%	305 100.0%	433 100.0%
Local problems				
Government	663 85.7%	524 94.8%	290 97.6%	333 83.8%
Individual	111 14.3%	28 5.2%	7 2.4%	64 16.2%
Total	775 100.0%	553 100.0%	297 100.0%	398 100.0%

TABLE 6.9 Government Versus Individual Role in Job Provision, by National Origin

Who Should Provide Jobs?	Mexican	Puerto Rican	Cuban	Anglo
Government should provide a job for everyone who needs one				
1	190	178	47	37
	21.6%	30.4%	15.0%	8.3%
2	73	56	20	36
	8.3%	9.6%	6.4%	8.1%
3	253	166	91	140
	28.9%	28.4%	29.2%	31.7%
4	91	27	22	83
	10.3%	4.6%	7.1%	18.7%
5	271	158	132	147
Individuals should get their own	30.9%	27.0%	42.3%	33.3%
Total	878	587	312	442
	100.0%	100.0%	100.0%	100.0%

Note: Respondents were asked to place themselves on a scale of one to five between the extreme positions stated.

TABLE 6.10 Government Versus Individual Role in Housing Provision, by National Origin

Who Should Provide Housing?	Mexican	Puerto Rican	Cuban	Anglo
Government should provide to people who need				
1	265	265	74	75
	30.2%	45.3%	23.8%	16.9%
2	99	75	41	62
	11.3%	12.8%	13.1%	13.9%
3	264	151	103	169
	30.1%	25.8%	33.0%	38.0%
4	68	25	26	52
	7.7%	4.2%	8.3%	11.7%
5	182	69	68	86
Individual should provide	20.7%	11.9%	21.8%	19.4%
Total	878	585	312	444
	100.0%	100.0%	100.0%	100.0%

Note: Respondents were asked to place themselves on a scale of one to five between the extreme positions stated.

TABLE 6.11 Government Versus Individual Role in Assuring Minimum Income, by National Origin

Who Should Provide Minimum Income?	*Mexican*	*Puerto Rican*	*Cuban*	*Anglo*
Government should provide, if needed				
1	179	141	49	46
	20.4%	24.1%	15.8%	10.5%
2	68	57	29	43
	7.8%	9.8%	9.2%	9.7%
3	234	183	99	146
	26.7%	31.2%	31.7%	33.2%
4	116	43	33	83
	13.2%	7.3%	10.7%	18.9%
5	280	161	101	122
Individual should provide	31.9%	27.6%	32.5%	27.7%
Total	876	585	312	441
	100.0%	100.0%	100.0%	100.0%

Note: Respondents were asked to place themselves on a scale of one to five between the extreme positions stated.

7

Public Policy Perspectives
of U.S. Citizens

This chapter focuses on a broad range of public policy issues facing American society. We assess Latino and, in many cases, Anglo positions on (1) issues facing the nation and the respondent's community; (2) attitudes toward government spending; (3) perceptions of discrimination; (4) language and cultural policy; (5) immigration policy; (6) foreign policy; (7) gender issues; and (8) other public policy issues.

The issue positions of these populations are not easily categorized in terms of a traditional liberal-conservative scale. On a broad range of public policy issues, they call for increased government involvement, even at the cost of higher taxes on themselves. On a range of issues such as abortion and affirmative action, however, they take more moderate or conservative positions. On language policy, they support the right to use Spanish, but they also expect all citizens and residents of the United States to learn English. Even though many are immigrants or the children of immigrants, majorities say that there are too many immigrants coming to the United States. Thus, instead of simplistically categorizing these populations as liberal or conservative, it is important to look at their beliefs on an issue-by-issue basis to understand the complexity of their views.

A. Public Policy Concerns (Tables 7.1 and 7.2)

Findings

The majority of Latinos, regardless of national origin, identified social problems as the most-important issues facing the nation (Table 7.1). For all Latino national-origin groups, as well as for Anglos, economic issues, such as employment, were identified as the second-most-important problem facing the nation.

Social issues, such as crime and drug control, also dominated at the local level (Table 7.2). At the local level, however, the majority of Anglos join the majority of the Latino national-origin groups in raising social issues. Again, Puerto Ricans saw the importance of social issues at higher rates (82 percent) than did Cubans (72 percent), Anglos (61 percent), or Mexicans (58 percent).

Questions Asked
109 and 111.

TABLE 7.1 Most-Important National Problem, by National Origin

Principal National Problem	Mexican	Puerto Rican	Cuban	Anglo
Economics	172	60	52	81
	22.7%	11.4%	17.8%	20.0%
Social problems	427	386	187	179
	56.3%	72.6%	63.7%	44.3%
Health care issues	26	7	8	32
	3.5%	1.2%	2.8%	7.9%
Education	20	12	14	9
	2.6%	2.3%	4.8%	2.3%
Immigration	1	3	3	5
	0.1%	0.6%	0.9%	1.1%
Political issues	29	13	11	11
	3.9%	2.5%	3.8%	2.7%
Environmental issues	20	3	4	32
	2.7%	0.6%	1.5%	7.9%
Ethnic issues	29	24	4	20
	3.8%	4.6%	1.3%	4.8%
Moral issues	25	15	7	21
	3.3%	2.8%	2.3%	5.3%
Others	9	7	4	14
	1.1%	1.4%	1.2%	3.6%
Total	758	532	294	404
	100.0%	100.0%	100.0%	100.0%

TABLE 7.2 Most-Important Local Problem, by National Origin

Principal Local Problem	Mexican	Puerto Rican	Cuban	Anglo
Economics	185	36	23	50
	24.7%	6.6%	7.7%	12.9%
Social issues	434	447	211	236
	58.0%	81.7%	72.4%	60.5%
Health care issues	4	7	0	9
	0.6%	1.3%	0.0%	2.2%
Education	26	15	9	11
	3.5%	2.7%	3.1%	2.8%
Immigration	1	0	14	4
	.2%	0.0%	4.8%	1.1%
Political issues	10	7	5	4
	1.4%	1.3%	1.7%	1.1%
Environmental issues	32	6	3	30
	4.3%	1.1%	1.1%	7.8%
Ethnic issues	28	17	10	12
	3.8%	3.1%	3.6%	3.2%
Moral issues	3	4	1	12
	0.4%	0.7%	0.3%	3.0%
Others	25	8	15	21
	3.3%	1.5%	5.2%	5.3%
Total	748	547	292	390
	100.0%	100.0%	100.0%	100.0%

B. Attitudes Toward Government Spending (Tables 7.3 and 7.4)

Findings

On a broad range of domestic issues—crime and drugs, education, health, child services, the environment—the majority of Latinos believed that federal spending should increase, even if it necessitated an increase in their taxes (Table 7.3). Puerto Ricans were more likely than either Mexicans or Cubans to call for increased spending on government programs. In addition to the policy areas just mentioned, the majority of Puerto Ricans expressed a willingness to pay more in taxes to fund increases in welfare spending. Despite the fact that the LNPS was conducted before the collapse of the Soviet Union, relatively few Latinos saw a need for increased defense expenditure.

Where the majority of Puerto Rican and Mexican respondents saw a need for increased government expenditure for programs to assist blacks, the majority of Cubans and Anglos did not (Table 7.4). A small majority of Cubans joined Puerto Ricans in calling for increased funding for refugee and legal immigrant support programs. Few Anglos (16 percent) and 41 percent of Mexicans saw a need for increased refugee-related expenditures.

Questions Asked

125a, 125b, 125c, 125d, 125e, 125f, 125g, 125h, 125i, and 125k.

TABLE 7.3   Attitudes Toward Increased Government Spending on Public Policy Areas, by National Origin

Government Spending Should Increase On:	Mexican	Puerto Rican	Cuban
Crime control and drug prevention	777 88.6% (n=877)	544 92.9% (n=585)	282 90.3% (n=312)
Public education	727 82.8% (n=878)	515 87.7% (n=587)	228 73.1% (n=312)
Health care	668 76.4% (n=874)	492 84.7% (n=580)	226 72.7% (n=311)
Child care services	583 66.5% (n=876)	455 77.5% (n=587)	214 68.6% (n=312)
Improving the environment	569 64.9% (n=878)	414 70.5% (n=587)	205 65.8% (n=312)
Public assistance/welfare	339 38.6% (n=877)	295 50.4% (n=585)	101 32.4% (n=312)
Support for science and technology	382 43.5% (n=877)	273 47.3% (n=577)	145 46.5% (n=312)
Defense	170 19.5% (n=876)	146 25.0% (n=583)	88 28.3% (n=312)

TABLE 7.4   Attitude Toward Increased Government Spending on Black Issues
and on Refugee and Legal Immigrant Services, by National Origin

Government Spending Should Increase On:	Mexican	Puerto Rican	Cuban	Anglo
Programs to help blacks	472	395	122	105
	53.7%	67.4%	39.2%	23.5%
	(n=878)	(n=587)	(n=312)	(n=446)
Programs for refugees and legal immigrants	361	326	160	73
	41.1%	56.1%	51.3%	16.4%
	(n=878)	(n=580)	(n=312)	(n=445)

C. Perceptions of Discrimination (Tables 7.5 - 7.14)

Findings

Regardless of national origin, the majority of Latino respondents reported that they had not been discriminated against because of their ethnicity (Table 7.5). It is noteworthy that Cubans were the least likely and Mexicans the most likely to report discriminatory experiences.

Although the majority of respondents had not had contact with public officials in the twelve months prior to being interviewed, almost all respondents who did have government contacts reported that they were treated as well as anyone else (Table 7.6). This perception of equal treatment included contacts with both Anglo and co-ethnic government officials (Table 7.7).

When asked about the level of discrimination experienced by several ethnic, racial, or gender groups in American society, i.e. African Americans, Asian Americans, Mexican Americans, Cuban Americans, Puerto Ricans, Jewish Americans, and women, in all but one case the minority of respondents felt that these groups experienced "a lot" of discrimination (Tables 7.8 - 7.14). The group most likely to be mentioned as facing a lot of discrimination was African Americans. Second was Mexican Americans. Cubans were the least likely to perceive a lot of discrimination against any group.

While approximately one-third of Puerto Ricans and Mexicans saw a lot of discrimination against their co-ethnics, just 6 percent of Cuban Americans saw a lot of discrimination against other Cubans.

Questions Asked

69, 71, 149, 150a, 150b, 150c, 150d, 150e, 150f, and 150g.

TABLE 7.5   Personal Experience with Discrimination, by National Origin

Respondent Discriminated Against Because of National Origin	*Mexican*	*Puerto Rican*	*Cuban*
Yes	341	176	55
	38.8%	30.0%	17.8%
No	537	410	256
	61.2%	70.0%	82.2%
Total	877	587	312
	100.0%	100.0%	100.0%

TABLE 7.6   Experiences With Public Officials, by National Origin

Treatment by a Public Official	*Mexican*	*Puerto Rican*	*Cuban*	*Anglo*
Treated as well as anyone else	199	119	74	132
	91.5%	90.7%	92.3%	88.2%
Others treated better	19	12	6	18
	8.5%	9.3%	7.7%	11.8%
Total	218	131	80	150
	100.0%	100.0%	100.0%	100.0%

TABLE 7.7   Differences in Treatment by Anglo and Co-Ethnic Public Officials, by National Origin

	Mexican	*Puerto Rican*	*Cuban*
Treatment by Anglo Officials			
Provided equal treatment	145	87	53
	91.2%	88.8%	93.0%
Treated others better	14	11	4
	8.8%	11.2%	7.0%
Total	159	98	57
	100.0%	100.0%	100.0%
Treatment by Co-Ethnic Officials			
Provided equal treatment	50	28	14
	94.3%	96.6%	87.5%
Treated others better	3	1	2
	5.7%	3.4%	12.5%
Total	53	29	16
	100.0%	100.0%	100.0%

TABLE 7.8 Perception of Discrimination Against African Americans, by National Origin

Degree of Discrimination Against Blacks	Mexican	Puerto Rican	Cuban	Anglo
A lot	383	336	93	138
	43.6%	57.5%	29.9%	31.2%
Some	350	166	109	234
	39.9%	28.4%	35.0%	52.7%
A little	113	52	44	53
	12.9%	9.0%	14.3%	11.9%
None	32	30	65	19
	3.6%	5.1%	20.9%	4.3%
Total	877	584	312	444
	100.0%	100.0%	100.0%	100.0%

TABLE 7.9 Perception of Discrimination Against Asian Americans, by National Origin

Degree of Discrimination Against Asians	Mexican	Puerto Rican	Cuban	Anglo
A lot	134	81	14	70
	15.5%	14.0%	4.6%	15.9%
Some	379	219	109	231
	43.9%	37.9%	35.2%	52.3%
A little	232	174	74	105
	26.9%	30.1%	23.9%	23.7%
None	119	104	112	36
	13.7%	18.1%	36.3%	8.1%
Total	864	577	308	441
	100.0%	100.0%	100.0%	100.0%

TABLE 7.10 Perception of Discrimination Against Mexican Americans, by National Origin

Degree of Discrimination Against Mexican Americans	Mexican	Puerto Rican	Cuban	Anglo
A lot	281	209	74	99
	32.1%	36.1%	24.0%	22.3%
Some	419	228	119	211
	47.9%	39.3%	38.7%	47.4%
A little	131	91	53	101
	15.0%	15.7%	17.1%	22.8%
None	44	52	62	33
	5.1%	9.0%	20.3%	7.5%
Total	876	581	308	446
	100.0%	100.0%	100.0%	100.0%

TABLE 7.11 Perception of Discrimination Against Cuban Americans, by National Origin

Degree of Discrimination Against Cuban Americans	Mexican	Puerto Rican	Cuban	Anglo
A lot	191	127	20	91
	22.6%	21.8%	6.3%	21.4%
Some	401	214	127	207
	47.5%	36.6%	40.7%	48.7%
A little	187	156	59	94
	22.1%	26.7%	19.0%	22.3%
None	67	87	106	32
	7.9%	14.9%	34.0%	7.5%
Total	845	585	312	424
	100.0%	100.0%	100.0%	100.0%

TABLE 7.12 Perception of Discrimination Against Puerto Ricans, by National Origin

Degree of Discrimination Against Puerto Ricans	*Mexican*	*Puerto Rican*	*Cuban*	*Anglo*
A lot	163	203	35	87
	19.1%	34.8%	11.2%	20.1%
Some	430	229	130	207
	50.4%	39.3%	41.8%	47.7%
A little	170	101	60	103
	20.0%	17.4%	19.2%	23.7%
None	89	50	86	37
	10.5%	8.6%	27.8%	8.5%
Total	852	582	310	433
	100.0%	100.0%	100.0%	100.0%

TABLE 7.13 Perception of Discrimination Against Women, by National Origin

Degree of Discrimination Against Women	*Mexican*	*Puerto Rican*	*Cuban*	*Anglo*
A lot	212	180	39	80
	24.4%	30.8%	12.5%	18.2%
Some	314	194	84	199
	36.2%	33.2%	27.1%	45.1%
A little	194	130	73	118
	22.4%	22.2%	23.6%	26.7%
None	149	81	114	44
	17.1%	13.8%	36.7%	10.1%
Total	869	585	311	441
	100.0%	100.0%	100.0%	100.0%

TABLE 7.14 Perception of Discrimination Against Jewish Americans,
by National Origin

Degree of Discrimination Against Jewish Americans	Mexican	Puerto Rican	Cuban	Anglo
A lot	117	89	11	42
	13.7%	15.7%	3.7%	9.6%
Some	311	170	63	157
	36.3%	30.1%	20.4%	35.9%
A little	213	127	67	148
	24.8%	22.4%	21.7%	33.9%
None	217	181	168	90
	25.3%	31.9%	54.2%	20.6%
Total	858	567	309	437
	100.0%	100.0%	100.0%	100.0%

D. Language and Cultural Policy (Tables 7.15–7.22)

Findings

Slight majorities of each of the Latino national-origin groups disagreed with the proposition that English should be the official language of the United States (Table 7.15). In marked contrast, Anglos strongly supported establishing English as the official language (79 percent).

Anglos and Latinos alike agreed that government services should be provided in Spanish (Table 7.16).

Latinos and Anglos divided over whether businesses should be able to require the use of English in the workplace (Table 7.17). Large majorities of Latinos, regardless of national origin, opposed this proposition; a slight majority of Anglos supported it.

More than 90 percent of Latinos supported the proposition that citizens and residents of the United States should learn English (Table 7.18).

More than 80 percent of Latinos supported bilingual education (Table 7.19). By bilingual education, most meant learning both English and Spanish or learning English (Table 7.20). Few define bilingual education in terms of maintaining Spanish language and culture. Approximately 70 percent of Mexicans and Puerto Ricans and 54 percent of Cubans were willing to pay more taxes to pay for bilingual education (Table 7.21).

Unlike Mexicans and Cubans, the majority of Puerto Ricans (72 percent) believed that children should learn equal amounts of United States and Puerto Rican history (Table 7.22). A slight majority of Mexicans and more than two-thirds of Cubans believed that children should learn U.S. history exclusively or more U.S. history than Mexican or Cuban history.

Questions Asked

161a, 161b, 161c, 161d, 162, 163, 164, and 165.

TABLE 7.15 English as the Official Language, by National Origin

English Should Be the Official Language	Mexican	Puerto Rican	Cuban	Anglo
Strongly agree	116	66	33	198
	13.7%	12.1%	10.7%	45.6%
Agree	262	200	89	147
	30.7%	36.8%	29.3%	33.7%
Disagree	334	223	145	75
	39.2%	41.2%	47.5%	17.3%
Strongly disagree	140	54	38	15
	16.4%	10.0%	12.4%	3.4%
Total	852	543	304	435
	100.0%	100.0%	100.0%	100.0%

TABLE 7.16 Attitude Toward Public Service Provision in Spanish, by National Origin

Public Services Should Be Provided in Spanish	Mexican	Puerto Rican	Cuban	Anglo
Strongly agree	197	154	85	59
	22.9%	26.5%	28.1%	13.7%
Agree	579	390	202	244
	67.3%	67.2%	66.4%	56.9%
Disagree	71	31	15	85
	8.3%	5.4%	5.0%	19.8%
Strongly disagree	14	5	2	41
	1.6%	0.9%	0.5%	9.6%
Total	861	580	304	429
	100.0%	100.0%	100.0%	100.0%

TABLE 7.17 Attitudes Toward Requiring English in the Workplace, by National Origin

Businesses Can Require English During Working Hours	Mexican	Puerto Rican	Cuban	Anglo
Strongly agree	58 6.7%	19 3.4%	18 5.8%	84 19.4%
Agree	198 23.1%	122 21.8%	65 21.3%	150 34.6%
Disagree	459 53.5%	332 59.1%	166 54.2%	155 35.8%
Strongly disagree	144 16.7%	88 15.7%	57 18.8%	44 10.2%
Total	859 100.0%	561 100.0%	306 100.0%	433 100.0%

TABLE 7.18 U.S. Citizens and Residents Should Learn English, by National Origin

Citizens and Residents of the U.S. Should Learn English	Mexican	Puerto Rican	Cuban
Strongly agree	251 29.1%	142 25.0%	79 25.6%
Agree	537 62.3%	386 67.7%	206 66.8%
Disagree	62 7.2%	32 5.6%	19 6.1%
Strongly disagree	12 1.4%	10 1.7%	5 1.6%
Total	862 100.0%	569 100.0%	309 100.0%

TABLE 7.19   Attitude Toward Bilingual Education, by National Origin

Attitude Toward Bilingual Education	Mexican	Puerto Rican	Cuban
Strongly support	321	232	100
	37.1%	39.7%	32.3%
Support	368	278	174
	42.5%	47.5%	56.1%
Feel uncertain	113	42	19
	13.0%	7.2%	6.1%
Oppose	46	23	6
	5.3%	3.9%	1.9%
Strongly oppose	18	10	11
	2.1%	1.7%	3.5%
Total	866	585	310
	100.0%	100.0%	100.0%

TABLE 7.20   Objective of Bilingual Education, by National Origin

Objective of Bilingual Education	Mexican	Puerto Rican	Cuban
To learn English	119	67	32
	14.7%	11.9%	10.3%
To learn two languages	569	415	240
	70.3%	73.6%	77.3%
To maintain Spanish language/culture	74	45	15
	9.1%	7.9%	4.9%
Other	48	37	23
	5.9%	6.6%	7.5%
Total	809	564	310
	100.0%	100.0%	100.0%

TABLE 7.21   Willingness to Be Taxed for Bilingual Education, by National Origin

Willing to Pay More Taxes for Bilingual Education	Mexican	Puerto Rican	Cuban
No	266	174	142
	31.0%	30.0%	45.9%
Yes	592	406	167
	69.0%	70.0%	54.1%
Total	858	580	309
	100.0%	100.0%	100.0%

TABLE 7.22 What Type of History Students Should Study, by National Origin

Type of History	Mexican	Puerto Rican	Cuban
Only U.S. history	68	29	49
	7.8%	4.9%	15.7%
More U.S. than RG history	403	122	159
	46.1%	20.8%	50.9%
U.S. history and RG history equally	398	418	103
	45.4%	71.6%	32.9%
More RG than U.S. history	6	15	2
	0.7%	2.6%	0.5%
Only RG history	2	1	0
	0.2%	0.1%	0.0%
Total	875	585	312
	100.0%	100.0%	100.0%

E. Immigration Policy (Tables 7.23–7.25)

Findings

Majorities of all Latino national-origin groups, and Cubans in particular, disagreed with the proposition that preference should be given in immigration law to immigrants from Latin America (Table 7.23).

More than 65 percent of each of the Latino national-origin groups as well as Anglos believed that there were currently too many immigrants coming to the U.S. (Table 7.24).

A majority of Puerto Ricans, Mexicans, and Anglos believed that U.S. citizens should be hired over noncitizens (Table 7.25). Fifty-eight percent of Cubans opposed this position.

Questions Asked

167a, 167b, and 167c.

TABLE 7.23 Preference for Latin American Immigration, by National Origin

Preference Should Be Given to Latin American Immigrants	Mexican	Puerto Rican	Cuban
Strongly agree	58 7.2%	30 5.9%	27 8.9%
Agree	247 30.7%	158 31.2%	62 20.7%
Disagree	442 54.8%	268 53.1%	171 57.1%
Strongly disagree	59 7.3%	49 9.8%	40 13.3%
Total	807 100.0%	505 100.0%	300 100.0%

TABLE 7.24 Attitude Toward Volume of Current Immigration, by National Origin

There Are Too Many Immigrants	Mexican	Puerto Rican	Cuban	Anglo
Strongly agree	171 20.2%	96 18.5%	32 11.0%	129 30.5%
Agree	466 55.0%	318 60.9%	159 54.5%	183 43.3%
Disagree	194 22.9%	101 19.3%	95 32.5%	94 22.3%
Strongly disagree	16 1.9%	7 1.4%	6 2.0%	16 3.9%
Total	847 100.0%	523 100.0%	292 100.0%	422 100.0%

TABLE 7.25 Attitude Toward Job Preference for Citizens, by National Origin

U.S. Citizens Should Be Hired Over Noncitizens	Mexican	Puerto Rican	Cuban	Anglo
Strongly agree	129	58	27	87
	15.3%	11.3%	9.5%	21.6%
Agree	332	227	93	120
	39.4%	43.7%	32.5%	29.9%
Disagree	338	194	150	171
	40.1%	37.4%	52.3%	42.7%
Strongly disagree	45	40	16	23
	5.3%	7.6%	5.7%	5.8%
Total	842	518	286	401
	100.0%	100.0%	100.0%	100.0%

F. Foreign Policy (Tables 7.26–7.32)

Findings

Large majorities of Mexicans and Cubans and more than 55 percent of Puerto Ricans were more concerned with U.S. politics than with homeland politics (Table 7.26). Fifteen percent of Puerto Ricans, 4 percent of Cubans, and 2 percent of Mexicans identified more with the homeland politics than with the U.S. politics.

Unlike Anglos, majorities from each of the Latino national-origin groups opposed establishing diplomatic relations with Cuba (Table 7.27). Cubans felt this most strongly (67 percent). However, 60 percent of Puerto Ricans and 56 percent of Mexicans opposed recognizing Cuba's government.

More than two-thirds of all Latinos, including 69 percent of Puerto Ricans, 61 percent of Cubans, and 55 percent of Mexicans supported retaining Commonwealth status for Puerto Rico (Table 7.28). Opinions as to the future of Puerto Rico were more divided among Anglos, with a plurality favoring Commonwealth status. Anglos were the most likely of any group to support independence for Puerto Rico.

Most respondents saw corruption within Mexico as the cause of Mexico's problems (Table 7.29). Though Cubans were most likely to hold this belief (at 92 percent), more than 80 percent of Mexicans, Puerto Ricans, and Anglos attribute Mexico's problems to factors internal to Mexico.

While the majority of Mexicans said that the United States should be less involved in Central America, majorities among Cuban and Puerto Rican respondents felt that the United States should be more involved (Table 7.30).

Clear majorities of Mexicans and Puerto Ricans attributed unrest in Central America to poverty and the lack of human rights (Table 7.31). Cuban respondents evenly divided the blame between poverty/human rights and Cuban and Soviet interference.

Most respondents had neutral feelings toward other countries (Table 7.32). On this scale, this implies a lack of information about these countries. On a scale of 0 to 100, the median score given to most countries was 50. Important exceptions were Cubans' feelings toward Russia (15) and Nicaragua (25), Mexicans' feelings toward Mexico (75) and Cuba (40), and Puerto Ricans' feelings toward Puerto Rico (100) and Cuba (35). The median score given to the United States, regardless of national origin was 100.

Questions Asked

134, 135, 136 137, 138a, 138b, 138c, 138d, 138e, 138f, 138g, 138h, 138i, 138j, 147, and 148.

TABLE 7.26 Concern with U.S. or Homeland Politics, by National Origin

Focus of Concern	Mexican	Puerto Rican	Cuban
More with homeland	20	80	11
	2.4%	14.6%	3.7%
U.S. and homeland equally	68	164	60
	8.2%	30.0%	19.8%
More with U.S.	749	302	232
	89.5%	55.4%	76.5%
Total	837	545	303
	100.0%	100.0%	100.0%

TABLE 7.27 U.S. Establishment of Diplomatic Relations with Cuba, by National Origin

Should U.S. Establish Relations With Cuba?	Mexican	Puerto Rican	Cuban	Anglo
No	414	289	195	174
	56.3%	59.7%	66.5%	49.1%
Yes	320	195	98	180
	43.7%	40.3%	33.5%	50.9%
Total	734	484	293	354
	100.0%	100.0%	100.0%	100.0%

TABLE 7.28 Attitude Toward the Status of Puerto Rico, by National Origin

Preferred Status of Puerto Rico	Mexican	Puerto Rican	Cuban	Anglo
A state	175	152	94	88
	23.9%	27.1%	35.2%	26.4%
A commonwealth	406	389	163	160
	55.4%	69.4%	60.7%	47.9%
Independent	152	20	11	86
	20.7%	3.5%	4.1%	25.7%
Total	732	560	268	333
	100.0%	100.0%	100.0%	100.0%

TABLE 7.29 Causes of Problems in Mexico, by National Origin

Causes of Problems in Mexico	Mexican	Puerto Rican	Cuban	Anglo
U.S. policy	45	40	5	20
	5.5%	8.3%	1.9%	5.0%
U.S. policy and corruption in Mexico	76	45	17	34
	9.4%	9.2%	5.9%	8.6%
Mexican corruption	686	402	258	339
	85.1%	82.5%	92.2%	86.4%
Total	807	487	280	392
	100.0%	100.0%	100.0%	100.0%

TABLE 7.30 Attitude Toward U.S. Involvement in Central America, by National Origin

Level of U.S. Involvement in Central America	Mexican	Puerto Rican	Cuban
Should be more involved	332 38.7%	314 57.1%	216 70.7%
Should be less involved	526 61.3%	236 42.9%	90 29.3%
Total	858 100.0%	549 100.0%	305 100.0%

TABLE 7.31 Cause of Unrest in Central America, by National Origin

Cause of Unrest in Central America	Mexican	Puerto Rican	Cuban
Cuban interference	179 20.9%	149 26.3%	117 37.8%
Cuban interference and poverty/ lack of human rights	86 10.0%	101 17.9%	63 20.5%
Poverty/lack of human rights	590 69.0%	316 55.8%	129 41.8%
Total	855 100.0%	567 100.0%	310 100.0%

TABLE 7.32 Feelings Toward Other Nations, by National Origin—Median Score

Country	Mexican	Puerto Rican	Cuban	Anglo
Russia	50 (n=852)	50 (n=569)	15 (n=308)	50 (n=444)
Mexico	75 (n=875)	50 (n=575)	50 (n=309)	50 (n=442)
Puerto Rico	50 (n=841)	100 (n=584)	70 (n=311)	50 (n=432)
Japan	50 (n=841)	50 (n=567)	50 (n=303)	50 (n=440)
Nicaragua	45 (n=838)	50 (n=567)	25 (n=304)	35 (n=423)
The United Kingdom	50 (n=836)	50 (n=563)	70 (n=301)	75 (n=442)
Cuba	40 (n=844)	35 (n=575)	50 (n=309)	30 (n=441)
Venezuela	50 (n=804)	50 (n=563)	50 (n=300)	50 (n=415)
Israel	50 (n=825)	50 (n=564)	50 (n=303)	50 (n=438)
The United States	100 (n=878)	100 (n=587)	100 (n=312)	100 (n=446)

G. Gender Issues (Tables 7.33–7.35)

Findings

Latinos more than Anglos saw it as appropriate for women to be in the work force (Table 7.33). Interestingly, Mexican men were more likely to hold this position than were Mexican women. Puerto Rican and Cuban women were slightly more likely than Puerto Rican and Cuban men to advocate strongly the position that women are better off if they have careers or jobs.

Mexican and Puerto Rican men and women split over the question of whether men or women are more capable public officeholders during crisis (Table 7.34). Majorities took a middle position. Among those who did not take the middle position, however, Mexican and Puerto Rican women were more likely to answer "women" while Mexican and Puerto Rican men were more likely to answer "men." Among those Cuban men and women who answered that one of the genders was better in crisis than the other, more answered "men" than "women."

When asked who should care for the children, the most popular answer was the midpoint on a five-point scale (Table 7.35). Seventy percent of Cubans take took this middle position, compared to 51 percent of Puerto Ricans and 48 percent of Mexicans.

Nearly one-third of Mexicans, led by Mexican women, took the position that men should help care for the home and children, even if it limited their careers. Just 20 percent of Puerto Ricans and 12 percent of Cubans advocated the man's helping with the children.

Questions Asked

157, 158, and 159.

TABLE 7.33 Role of Women, by National Origin

Should Women Be in the Home or Have Careers?	Mexican		Puerto Rican		Cuban		Anglo	
	Female	Male	Female	Male	Female	Male	Female	Male
Women better off if they stay home and rear children								
1	72	64	46	45	27	32	35	20
	15.2%	15.8%	14.2%	17.4%	15.9%	22.9%	15.7%	9.3%
2	18	8	18	20	4	4	14	12
	3.8%	2.0%	5.6%	7.6%	2.3%	2.5%	6.2%	5.6%
3	159	121	90	87	66	36	87	84
	33.6%	30.0%	27.7%	33.3%	38.3%	25.8%	38.5%	39.4%
4	46	45	37	18	9	22	38	36
	9.7%	11.0%	11.3%	6.9%	5.5%	15.4%	16.8%	16.7%
5	178	166	135	91	65	47	51	62
Women better off if they have careers and jobs	37.7%	41.2%	41.2%	34.8%	37.9%	33.3%	22.8%	29.0%
Total	472	404	327	260	172	140	226	213
	100.0%	100.0%	100.0%	100.0%	100.0%	100.0%	100.0%	100.0%

Note: Respondents were asked to place themselves on a scale of one to five between the extreme positions stated.

TABLE 7.34   Attitude Toward Women in Public Office During Crises,
by National Origin

Women's Capability in Office During Crisis	Mexican		Puerto Rican		Cuban	
	Female	*Male*	*Female*	*Male*	*Female*	*Male*
Men more capable than women in public office during crisis						
1	67	96	41	67	39	39
	14.2%	23.7%	12.5%	25.6%	22.5%	27.8%
2	30	48	12	24	4	9
	6.3%	11.7%	3.7%	9.1%	2.2%	6.3%
3	275	214	189	129	105	84
	58.3%	52.7%	58.0%	49.8%	61.3%	59.7%
4	32	15	25	12	8	4
	6.9%	3.8%	7.7%	4.7%	4.5%	3.0%
5	68	33	59	28	16	4
Women more capable than men in public office during crisis	14.4%	8.1%	18.1%	10.7%	9.4%	3.2%
Total	471	406	326	260	171	140
	100.0%	100.0%	100.0%	100.0%	100.0%	100.0%

Note: Respondents were asked to place themselves on a scale of one to five between the extreme positions stated.

TABLE 7.35 Responsibility for Home and Children, by National Origin

Primary Caregiver	Mexican		Puerto Rican		Cuban	
	Female	Male	Female	Male	Female	Male
Even if it limits career, women should care for home and children						
1	44	52	45	35	20	14
	9.3%	12.8%	14.0%	13.6%	11.6%	9.8%
2	11	31	13	34	5	7
	2.4%	7.5%	3.9%	13.2%	2.8%	4.9%
3	227	194	181	119	123	96
	48.2%	48.0%	55.7%	45.6%	71.6%	68.6%
4	44	28	19	25	4	7
	9.4%	7.0%	5.7%	9.6%	2.5%	5.1%
5	145	100	68	47	20	16
Even if it limits career, men should care for home and children	30.7%	24.7%	20.8%	18.0%	11.5%	11.7%
Total	471	405	325	260	172	140
	100.0%	100.0%	100.0%	100.0%	100.0%	100.0%

Note: Respondents were asked to place themselves on a scale of one to five between the extreme positions stated.

H. Other Public Policy Issues (Tables 7.36–7.38)

Findings

While the majority of Cubans and Anglos believed that jobs and college admission should be based strictly on merit, Puerto Rican and Mexican opinion was more divided (Table 7.36). A slightly greater share of the Mexican respondents supported merit over quotas. This pattern was reversed in the Puerto Rican community.

Majorities in each of these populations supported capital punishment (Table 7.37). Support was stronger among Cubans and Mexicans than among Puerto Ricans.

The majority of Mexican women and Puerto Ricans, regardless of gender, held a restrictionist view of abortion (Table 7.38). Majorities of Mexican men and of Cuban men and women supported abortion in some or all cases.

Questions Asked

151, 155, and 160.

TABLE 7.36 Job and College Admission Quotas, by National Origin

Basis of Job and College Admission	Mexican	Puerto Rican	Cuban	Anglo
Government quotas				
1	168	139	37	8
	19.4%	24.0%	11.9%	1.7%
2	104	57	20	21
	11.9%	9.9%	6.3%	4.7%
3	262	202	56	93
	30.2%	34.8%	17.8%	21.1%
4	80	36	22	89
	9.3%	6.1%	7.0%	20.4%
5	255	147	177	228
Strictly merit	29.3%	25.2%	56.9%	52.0%
Total	869	581	312	439
	100.0%	100.0%	100.0%	100.0%

Note: Respondents were asked to place themselves on a scale of one to five between the extreme positions stated.

TABLE 7.37 Attitude Toward Capital Punishment, by National Origin

Opinion of Capital Punishment for Convicted Murderers	Mexican	Puerto Rican	Cuban
Support	570	308	214
	65.4%	53.1%	69.7%
Depends on the case	150	121	51
	17.2%	20.9%	16.6%
Opposition	152	152	42
	17.4%	26.1%	13.7%
Total	872	581	307
	100.0%	100.0%	100.0%

TABLE 7.38 Attitude Toward Abortion, by National Origin

Conditions Under Which Abortion Should Be Permitted	Mexican		Puerto Rican		Cuban	
	Female	Male	Female	Male	Female	Male
None	109	67	61	70	21	15
	23.3%	16.8%	18.6%	27.0%	12.0%	11.0%
Rape or incest	156	128	128	86	61	41
	33.3%	31.9%	39.0%	33.2%	35.8%	30.1%
Only if needed	43	53	37	39	25	34
	9.3%	13.2%	11.2%	15.1%	14.4%	25.1%
Any	160	153	102	64	65	46
	34.1%	38.1%	31.3%	24.8%	37.8%	33.9%
Total	469	401	327	260	172	136
	100.0%	100.0%	100.0%	100.0%	100.0%	100.0%

8

Organizational and Electoral Behavior of U.S. Citizens

This chapter describes organizational, governmental, and political behavior among Latinos and Anglos. We examine (1) organizational participation; (2) problem-solving strategies for public policy issues; and (3) partisanship and electoral behavior.

Significant minorities of Latinos engage in a diverse range of political and organizational activities. Between 37 percent and 57 percent are members of organizations. Twenty to 30 percent participate in political activities such as signing petitions or wearing campaign buttons. Many are involved in school-related activities. A majority are registered to vote.

Use of the franchise varies by national origin. Among Mexicans and Puerto Ricans, the nonregistered and the registered who failed to vote exceed the number of voters. Among Cubans and Anglos, twice as many respondents voted as did not vote or were ineligible to vote. Michael Dukakis carried the Mexican vote, George Bush carried the Cuban and Anglo votes, and the two candidates split the Puerto Rican vote, with a slight majority going to Bush.

A. Organizational Participation (Tables 8.1–8.4)

Findings

The type of organization named most frequently as looking out for respondents' concerns was national-origin-based (Table 8.1). Fifty-three percent of Mexicans, 57 percent of Puerto Ricans, and 68 percent of Cubans named this type of organization. For Mexican and Puerto Rican respondents, Latino/Hispanic organizations were the second-most-often-mentioned. Among Cubans, the second-most-often-mentioned organization type was religious or charitable.

Overall, Latinos participated in and contributed to organizations at lower rates than did Anglos (Tables 8.2 and 8.3). Among Latinos, Mexicans were most likely to belong and contribute to organizations.

Puerto Rican women had a more difficult time attending meetings than did Puerto Rican men (Table 8.4). Among Cubans and Mexicans, gender did not seem to influence the ability to attend meetings.

Questions Asked

55a, 55b, 55c, 56a, 56b, 56c, 57a, 57b, 57c, 58a, 58b, 58c, 61, 62, 63, 64, and 105.

TABLE 8.1 Organizations That Represent Respondent, by National Origin

Types of Organizations That Represent Respondent	Mexican	Puerto Rican	Cuban
National-origin	465	332	212
	53.0%	56.6%	67.9%
Pan-ethnic (Latino/Hispanic)	57	24	11
	6.5%	4.1%	3.5%
Work or business	17	4	5
	1.9%	0.7%	1.6%
Religious or charitable	31	8	13
	3.5%	1.4%	4.2%
Social issues or advocacy	15	7	6
	1.7%	1.2%	1.9%
Youth, sports, or community	36	22	2
	4.1%	3.7%	0.6%
Government-related	25	9	3
	2.8%	1.5%	1.0%
None	232	182	60
	26.4%	31.0%	19.2%
Total	878	587	312
	100.0%	100.0%	100.0%

TABLE 8.2 Membership in Organizations, by National Origin

Type of Organization	Mexican	Puerto Rican	Cuban	Anglo
Work-related	147	61	50	117
	16.7%	10.4%	16.0%	26.2%
Charitable	270	106	99	173
	30.8%	18.1%	31.7	38.8%
Social	31	20	33	81
	3.5%	3.4%	10.6%	18.2%
Sports	138	49	55	115
	15.7%	8.3%	17.6%	25.8%
None	377	368	147	110
	42.9%	62.7%	47.1%	24.7%
Total respondents	878	587	312	446
	100.0%	100.0%	100.0%	100.0%

Note: Respondents may hold multiple memberships. Therefore, the number of memberships is greater than the total number of respondents.

TABLE 8.3 Contributions to Organizations, by National Origin

Type of Organization to Which Financial Contribution Is Made	Mexican	Puerto Rican	Cuban	Anglo
Work-related	159	56	57	121
	18.1%	9.5%	18.3%	27.1%
Charitable	650	208	227	532
	74.0%	35.4%	72.8%	119.3%
Social	70	23	45	137
	8.0%	3.9%	14.4%	30.7%
Sports	205	60	62	177
	23.3%	10.2%	19.9%	39.7%
None	377	367	147	110
	42.9%	62.5%	47.1%	24.7%
Total respondents	878	587	312	446
	100.0%	100.0%	100.0%	100.0%

Note: Respondents may contribute to multiple organizations. Therefore, the number of contributors is greater than the total number of respondents.

TABLE 8.4   Ability to Attend Meetings, by National Origin and Gender

Degree of Difficulty in Attending Meetings	Mexican		Puerto Rican		Cuban	
	Female	*Male*	*Female*	*Male*	*Female*	*Male*
Very difficult	45	24	54	38	29	19
	8.6%	6.8%	16.0%	15.6%	16.0%	15.2%
Somewhat difficult	105	71	103	47	37	24
	20.1%	20.1%	30.5%	19.0%	19.9%	18.9%
Not difficult	373	259	181	160	118	84
	71.3%	73.1%	53.5%	65.4%	64.2%	65.9%
Total	524	354	337	246	184	128
	100.0%	100.0%	100.0%	100.0%	100.0%	100.0%

B. Problem-Solving Strategies for Public Policy Issues (Tables 8.5–8.12)

Findings

Approximately three-quarters of Latino respondents had not contacted a government agency within the twelve months prior to being interviewed (Table 8.5). Among those who had, questions relating to government services and the clarification of regulations were the two most-important reasons for governmental contact.

Respondents who contacted government in an effort to solve a problem were very likely to be satisfied with the experience (Table 8.6).

More than four-fifths of respondents had not engaged in collective action to solve a community problem in the year before being interviewed by the LNPS (Table 8.7). Among the few mentioning public policy problems addressed through collective action, the most-often mentioned were social issues such as crime or drugs.

Collective problem-solving efforts, for the most part, did not involve RG issues (Table 8.8). This was particularly true among the Cuban respondents.

Mexican and Puerto Rican respondents were three times as likely to be satisfied as dissatisfied with the results of collective action (Table 8.9). Among Cubans, the very satisfied outnumbered the very dissatisfied by a factor of seven.

Among those who tried to solve the identified problems, many more acted collectively than either contacted government officials or acted on their own to solve the problem (Table 8.10).

Respondents reported low levels of involvement in a variety of political activities (Table 8.11). Despite the fact that they voted at lower levels than Cuban respondents, Mexican respondents participated at higher levels in five of these seven activities (Table 8.18).

More than half of Mexican and Puerto Rican and 40 percent of Cuban respondents engaged in school-related activities (Table 8.12). The most often mentioned were meeting with a teacher and attending PTA meetings. The least-frequently mentioned activity was attending a school board meeting.

Questions Asked

65, 66, 70, 106a, 106b, 106c, 106d, 106e, 119, 120, 121, 122, 123, 124a, 124b, 124c, 124d, 124e, 124f, and 124g.

TABLE 8.5 Reasons for Visiting Government Office, by National Origin

Reason for Government Contact During Twelve Months Before Interview	Mexican	Puerto Rican	Cuban	Anglo
Clarify regulations	53	24	23	54
	6.1%	4.1%	7.3%	12.3%
Immigration	7	1	10	0
	.8%	.2%	3.2%	0.0%
Services	91	72	24	43
	10.4%	12.4%	7.7%	9.8%
Employment	35	9	6	11
	4.0%	1.6%	2.0%	2.4%
Other	31	23	17	39
	3.5%	4.0%	5.6%	8.8%
No government contacts	655	451	230	294
	75.2%	77.8%	74.2%	66.7%
Total	872	580	310	441
	100.0%	100.0%	100.0%	100.0%

TABLE 8.6 Satisfaction Among Those Who Contacted Government, by National Origin

Satisfaction With Government Contact	Mexican	Puerto Rican	Cuban
Very satisfied	86 39.1%	40 29.6%	31 38.8%
Satisfied	83 37.7%	69 51.1%	30 37.5%
Not satisfied	51 23.2%	26 19.3%	19 23.8%
Total	220 100.0%	135 100.0%	80 100.0%

TABLE 8.7 Cooperative Efforts at Problem Solving, by National Origin

Problem Type	Mexican	Puerto Rican	Cuban	Anglo
Economic	4 0.4%	10 1.7%	3 1.1%	1 0.1%
Social	88 10.2%	53 9.1%	24 7.8%	46 10.5%
Health	4 0.4%	3 0.5%	3 0.8%	0 0.1%
Education	15 1.8%	2 0.3%	0 0.0%	2 0.5%
Political	19 2.2%	11 1.8%	3 1.0%	11 2.5%
Environment	9 1.0%	9 1.5%	2 0.6%	20 4.6%
Ethnic	4 0.5%	3 0.5%	0 0.0%	1 0.2%
Moral	1 0.1%	1 0.2%	1 0.3%	5 1.1%
Other	10 1.1%	6 1.0%	1 0.3%	17 3.8%
None	713 82.3%	487 83.4%	272 88.1%	340 76.7%
Total	867 100.0%	584 100.0%	309 100.0%	443 100.0%

TABLE 8.8 Impact on RGs of Collectively Addressed Problem, by National Origin

Did the Collectively Addressed Problem Affect RGs?	Mexican	Puerto Rican	Cuban
Yes	58	40	8
	35.2%	40.0%	20.5%
No	107	60	31
	64.8%	60.0%	79.5%
Total	165	100	39
	100.0%	100.0%	100.0%

TABLE 8.9 Satisfaction Among Those Who Participated, With the Results of Collective Action, by National Origin

Degree of Satisfaction	Mexican	Puerto Rican	Cuban
Very satisfied	58	29	23
	35.4%	29.3%	57.5%
Satisfied	64	45	12
	39.0%	45.5%	30.0%
Unsatisfied	29	23	2
	17.7%	23.2%	5.0%
Very unsatisfied	13	2	3
	7.9%	2.0%	7.5%
Total	164	99	40
	100.0%	100.0%	100.0%

TABLE 8.10 Action Taken to Solve Local Problems, by National Origin

Type of Action Taken	Mexican	Puerto Rican	Cuban	Anglo
None	711	482	272	336
	81.3%	83.3%	88.8%	76.9%
Contacted government	33	12	3	19
	3.8%	2.1%	1.1%	4.3%
Acted with others	97	53	27	69
	11.1%	9.1%	8.9%	15.8%
Acted autonomously	34	32	3	13
	3.9%	5.5%	1.1%	3.0%
Total	875	579	307	437
	100.0%	100.0%	100.0%	100.0%

TABLE 8.11 Participation in Political Activities, by National Origin

Activity	Mexican	Puerto Rican	Cuban	Anglo
Signed a petition	262	121	74	220
	29.9%	20.7%	23.8%	49.4%
	(n=877)	(n=587)	(n=311)	(n=446)
Wrote to the press	106	53	45	90
	12.1%	9.1%	14.4%	20.2%
	(n=878)	(n=587)	(n=312)	(n=445)
Attended a public meeting	156	97	39	94
	17.7%	16.6%	12.4%	21.1%
	(n=878)	(n=587)	(n=312)	(n=446)
Wore a campaign button	157	105	57	97
	17.9%	17.8%	18.1%	21.7%
	(n=878)	(n=587)	(n=312)	(n=446)
Went to rallies	80	47	28	41
	9.1%	7.9%	8.9%	9.2%
	(n=878)	(n=587)	(n=312)	(n=446)
Volunteered for a political party	61	26	14	20
	7.0%	4.4%	4.5%	4.6%
	(n=878)	(n=587)	(n=312)	(n=446)
Made political contributions	79	38	22	56
	9.0%	6.4%	7.0%	12.6%
	(n=877)	(n=587)	(n=312)	(n=446)

TABLE 8.12 Involvement With Schools, by National Origin

Activity	Mexican	Puerto Rican	Cuban	Anglo
Met with teacher	546	327	122	
	62.5%	55.6%	39.3%	a
	(n=874)	(n=587)	(n=312)	
Attended a PTA meeting	365	237	94	210
	41.8%	40.4%	30.1%	47.1%
	(n=875)	(n=587)	(n=311)	(n=446)
Met with school principal	417	253	97	240
	47.6%	43.0%	31.4%	54.0%
	(n=875)	(n=587)	(n=311)	(n=445)
Attended a school board meeting	158	118	42	88
	18.1%	20.2%	13.6%	19.8%
	(n=875)	(n=587)	(n=311)	(n=446)
Voted in a school board election	245	124	48	192
	28.1%	21.2%	15.3%	43.1%
	(n=872)	(n=586)	(n=311)	(n=446)

a=Not asked of Anglos.

C. Partisanship and Electoral Behavior (Tables 8.13–8.27)

Findings

More than three-quarters of respondents have been registered to vote at some point in their lives (Table 8.13) and between 64 percent and 78 percent were registered at the time of the interview (Table 8.14). Voter registration rates among Cubans and Anglos were 78 percent; among Mexicans and Puerto Ricans, respectively, they were 65 percent and 64 percent.

Most respondents were not contacted by others, such as voter-registration drives, to register in 1988 (Table 8.15). This absence of contact by voter-registration campaigns was particularly marked in the Cuban community, where just 21 percent were contacted to register.

The minority of respondents have been contacted to register and vote (Table 8.16). Mexicans were twice as likely as Cubans to be contacted to register.

Almost half of Mexicans and Puerto Ricans, nearly 70 percent of Cubans, and more than 70 percent of Anglos voted in the 1988 election (Table 8.17).

In the Mexican and Puerto Rican communities, the nonregistered or the registered who failed to vote exceeded the number of voters in 1988 (Table 8.18). Among Cubans and Anglos, on the other hand, twice as many respondents voted as either did not vote or were ineligible to vote.

Among those who did vote, Michael Dukakis carried the Mexican vote 62 percent to 37 percent, George Bush carried the Cuban and Anglo votes 86 percent to 14 percent and 55 percent to 43 percent, respectively, and the two candidates split the Puerto Rican vote, with a slight majority going to Bush (50 percent to 47 percent).

George Bush was the favorite candidate of the nonvoters, regardless of national origin (Table 8.19). This preference for Bush among the nonvoters was strongest among Cubans and weakest among Mexican and Puerto Rican respondents. Anglos fell in between these extremes.

Congressional voting followed the patterns for presidential turnout (Table 8.20). The majority of Cubans and Anglos voted in the 1988 congressional race, at rates of 54 percent and 61 percent, respectively. The majority of Puerto Ricans and Mexicans did not vote in the congressional race (69 percent and 61 percent, respectively).

Mexicans, Puerto Ricans, and Anglos were more likely to vote for Democratic than Republican congressional candidates in 1988 (Table 8.21). Cubans were approximately four times as likely to vote for Republican as Democrat congressional candidates.

Among Spanish-dominant U.S. citizens, the majority of Mexicans and Cubans had access to Spanish-language ballots (Table 8.22). Forty-seven percent of Puerto Ricans had similar access. Among those Spanish-dominant U.S. citizens who had access to bilingual election materials in 1988, 62 percent of Mexicans, 73 percent of Puerto Ricans, and 77 percent of Cubans used the Spanish materials.

The majority of respondents who were U.S. citizens in 1984 reported that they voted in that year's presidential elections (Table 8.23). If respondents' memories accurately reflect their voting patterns, this suggests a sometimes significant drop-off in voter turnout between 1984 and 1988. This drop-off is greatest among Mexican respondents (from 55.4 percent in 1984 to 49.3% in 1988).

More than two-thirds of Mexican and Puerto Rican respondents identified as or leaned toward the Democrats and more than two-thirds of Cuban respondents identified or leaned towards the Republicans (Table 8.24). Anglos were more evenly divided with 50 percent allied with the Democrats and 40 percent allied with the Republicans.

The Republican party identifiers included a significant portion who have shifted their allegiance from the Democratic party (Table 8.25). More than one-third of Mexican Republicans, one-fifth of Puerto Rican Republicans, and one-sixth of Cuban Republicans were former Democrats. The partisan allegiances and loyalty of Anglo Republicans were comparable to those of the Mexican Republicans. Few Republicans had become Democrats.

Respondents' descriptions of what the parties stand for suggest that the majority had an understanding of the parties (Tables 8.26 and 8.27). For both parties, Puerto Rican respondents were most likely not to know what the parties stood for.

Questions Asked

72, 73, 74, 75, 78, 79, 80, 81, 82, 83, 84, 85, 87, 91, 92, 93, 94, 95, 96, 97, 98, 99, 100, 101, and 102.

TABLE 8.13 Voter Registration, by National Origin

Has Respondent Ever Registered to Vote?	Mexican	Puerto Rican	Cuban	Anglo
No	201	154	55	45
	22.9%	26.3%	17.7%	10.0%
Yes	676	431	256	401
	77.1%	73.7%	82.3%	90.0%
Total	877	585	312	446
	100.0%	100.0%	100.0%	100.0%

TABLE 8.14 Current Voter Registration Status, by National Origin

Respondent Registered to Vote in 1989-1990	Mexican	Puerto Rican	Cuban	Anglo
No	303	211	69	99
	34.6%	36.0%	22.0%	22.2%
Yes	574	375	243	347
	65.4%	64.0%	78.0%	77.8%
Total	877	585	312	446
	100.0%	100.0%	100.0%	100.0%

TABLE 8.15 Voter Registration Outreach, by National Origin

Respondent Contacted to Register in 1988	Mexican	Puerto Rican	Cuban	Anglo
No	519	385	247	275
	60.0%	65.9%	79.5%	62.9%
Yes	346	199	64	163
	40.0%	34.1%	20.5%	37.1%
Total	865	584	310	438
	100.0%	100.0%	100.0%	100.0%

TABLE 8.16 Who Contacted Respondent to Register to Vote, by National Origin

Who Contacted Respondent to Register	Mexican	Puerto Rican	Cuban
Family and friends	39	35	4
	4.5%	6.1%	1.3%
Social and professional associates	45	24	9
	5.2%	4.2%	2.9%
Public officials	54	25	16
	6.2%	4.3%	5.2%
Registrar	49	26	6
	5.7%	4.5%	1.9%
Other	159	83	27
	18.4%	14.4%	8.7%
Nobody	519	385	247
	60.0%	66.6%	79.9%
Total	865	578	309
	100.0%	100.0%	100.0%

TABLE 8.17 Voting in 1988 Presidential Election, by National Origin

Did Respondent Vote in the 1988 Election?	Mexican	Puerto Rican	Cuban	Anglo
Yes	431	290	210	313
	49.3%	49.9%	67.2%	70.2%
No	141	81	34	34
	16.1%	13.9%	10.7%	7.6%
Not registered	303	211	69	99
	34.6%	36.2%	22.0%	22.2%
Total	875	581	312	446
	100.0%	100.0%	100.0%	100.0%

TABLE 8.18 Candidate Preference in 1988 Election, by National Origin

Candidate Preference	Mexican	Puerto Rican	Cuban	Anglo
George Bush	152	143	177	167
	17.5%	24.6%	56.9%	37.5%
Michael Dukakis	259	134	28	131
	29.8%	23.2%	9.0%	29.5%
Another candidate	5	7	0	5
	0.5%	1.1%	0.1%	1.2%
Voted in other 1988 elections	7	4	4	2
	0.8%	0.7%	1.2%	0.4%
Not registered	303	211	69	99
	34.8%	36.3%	22.1%	22.2%
Did not vote	141	81	34	34
	16.2%	13.9%	10.8%	7.6%
Refused to answer	3	2	0	7
	0.4%	0.3%	0.0%	1.7%
Total	871	580	311	446
	100.0%	100.0%	100.0%	100.0%

TABLE 8.19 Preferred Presidential Candidate of Nonvoters, 1988, by National Origin

Candidate	Mexican	Puerto Rican	Cuban	Anglo
George Bush	160	109	63	63
	36.5%	42.0%	67.1%	52.2%
Michael Dukakis	124	72	8	22
	28.3%	27.5%	9.0%	18.5%
Another candidate	155	79	23	36
	35.2%	30.5%	23.9%	29.3%
Total	439	260	94	122
	100.0%	100.0%	100.0%	100.0%

TABLE 8.20 Congressional Voting, 1988, by National Origin

Did Respondent Vote in 1988 U.S. House Election?	Mexican	Puerto Rican	Cuban	Anglo
Yes	327	167	152	248
	39.1%	31.4%	54.0%	60.8%
No	64	75	27	27
	7.7%	14.1%	9.4%	6.6%
Not registered	303	211	69	99
	36.3%	39.5%	24.4%	24.2%
Did not vote	141	81	34	34
	16.9%	15.1%	11.9%	8.3%
Refused to answer	0	0	1	0
	0.0%	0.0%	0.2%	0.0%
Total	835	533	281	408
	100.0%	100.0%	100.0%	100.0%

TABLE 8.21 Party Supported in 1988 Congressional Vote, by National Origin

Party	Mexican	Puerto Rican	Cuban	Anglo
Republican	74	55	118	107
	22.6%	32.9%	77.6%	43.1%
Democrat	238	103	31	126
	72.8%	61.7%	20.4%	50.8%
Another party or cannot remember	14	9	3	14
	4.3%	5.4%	2.0%	5.6%
Refused to answer	1	0	0	1
	0.3%	0.0%	0.0%	0.4%
Total	327	167	152	248
	100.0%	100.0%	100.0%	100.0%

TABLE 8.22 Availability and Use of Spanish Language Assistance and Voting Materials by Spanish-Dominant U.S. Citizens Who Voted in 1988, by National Origin

Availability and Use of Assistance and Voting Materials	Mexican	Puerto Rican	Cuban
Assistance and Materials Available to Spanish-Dominant Voters			
Spanish-language ballots available	52	77	106
	69.3%	47.5%	74.1%
	(n=75)	(n=162)	(n=143)
Election official provided assistance in Spanish at the polls	15	39	21
	20.0%	24.1%	14.7%
	(n=75)	(n=162)	(n=143)
Use of Spanish Language Voting Materials			
Used Spanish or combination of Spanish and English ballots	32	56	82
	61.5%	72.7%	77.4%
	(n=52)	(n=77)	(n=106)
Spanish-language ballots have helped respondent vote	37	59	69
	49.3%	36.4%	48.3%
	(n=75)	(n=162)	(n=143)

Note: These questions were asked only of U.S. citizens who answered the LNPS in Spanish and who voted in the 1988 elections.

TABLE 8.23 Presidential Voting in 1984, by National Origin

Voted in the 1984 Presidential Election	Mexican	Puerto Rican	Cuban
No	321	243	76
	44.6%	49.2%	28.5%
Yes	398	251	191
	55.4%	50.8%	71.5%
Total	720	493	267
	100.0%	100.0%	100.0%

TABLE 8.24 Partisan Identification, by National Origin

Party Identification	Mexican	Puerto Rican	Cuban	Anglo
Strong Democrat	252	205	45	78
	31.0%	37.2%	14.4%	17.8%
Not strong Democrat	232	145	16	113
	28.6%	26.4%	5.1%	25.9%
Closer to Democrat	59	40	18	40
	7.2%	7.4%	6.0%	9.2%
Independent/other	94	63	18	31
	11.5%	11.5%	5.7%	7.1%
Closer to Republican	45	20	15	48
	5.5%	3.6%	4.8%	11.0%
Not strong Republican	94	40	50	58
	11.6%	7.2%	16.2%	13.4%
Strong Republican	36	37	147	68
	4.4%	6.7%	47.8%	15.7%
Total	811	550	309	436
	100.0%	100.0%	100.0%	100.0%

TABLE 8.25 Party Loyalty, by National Origin

Partisan Loyalty	Mexican	Puerto Rican	Cuban	Anglo
Republican Party Loyalty				
Always Republican	81	55	159	74
	64.3%	79.7%	82.4%	64.9%
Former Democrat	45	14	34	40
	35.7%	20.3%	17.6%	35.1%
Total	126	69	193	114
	100.0%	100.0%	100.0%	100.0%
Democrat Partisan Loyalty				
Always Democrat	468	330	56	171
	97.5%	95.4%	96.6%	92.9%
Former Republican	12	16	2	13
	2.5%	4.6%	3.4%	7.1%
Total	480	346	58	184
	100.0%	100.0%	100.0%	100.0%

TABLE 8.26 Agreement With Republican Party Characterization,
by National Origin

Degree of Agreement With Characterization	Mexican	Puerto Rican	Cuban	Anglo
Agree	512	257	188	298
	58.4%	43.8%	60.2%	66.8%
Disagree	91	56	32	37
	10.3%	9.5%	10.2%	8.2%
Neither agree nor disagree	75	76	48	48
	8.5%	12.9%	15.2%	10.7%
Don't know	200	199	45	64
	22.8%	33.9%	14.3%	14.3%
Total	878	587	312	446
	100.0%	100.0%	100.0%	100.0%

TABLE 8.27 Agreement With Democratic Party Characterization, by National Origin

Degree of Agreement With Characterization	*Mexican*	*Puerto Rican*	*Cuban*	*Anglo*
Agree	499	277	147	271
	56.8%	47.2%	47.0%	60.9%
Disagree	50	26	51	40
	5.7%	4.4%	16.2%	8.9%
Neither agree nor disagree	143	106	65	66
	16.3%	18.0%	21.0%	14.9%
Don't know	186	178	49	68
	21.2%	30.4%	15.8%	15.2%
Total	878	587	312	446
	100.0%	100.0%	100.0%	100.0%

9

Ethnic Attitudes and Behaviors of U.S. Citizens

This chapter reviews attitudes toward ethnicity, both among RGs, that is, people sharing the same national origin, and among all Latinos. We examine six aspects of ethnicity: (1) perceptions of ethnic mutual support; (2) ethnic organizational behavior; (3) ethnic electoral behavior; (4) interest in and knowledge of national-origin-based activities; (5) public policy problems facing Latino communities; and (6) perceptions of common ethnic bonds among Latinos.

While most respondents perceived that there were commonalities among co-ethnics, fewer saw this commonality extending beyond national-origin groups to include all Latinos. Despite this feeling of solidarity with other co-ethnics, few respondents were involved in organizations or political activities that foster the development of ethnic unity.

A. Perceptions of Ethnic Mutual Support (Tables 9.1–9.4)

Findings

Fewer Cubans (55 percent) believed that they had an obligation to help their co-ethnics than did Puerto Ricans (73 percent) or Mexicans (71 percent) (Table 9.1).

The majority of Mexicans, Cubans, and Puerto Ricans believed that members of one's own nationality group helped each other (Table 9.2). The perception was much stronger among Cubans than among the other national-origin groups.

Majorities of each group believed that they benefited when other Cubans, Mexicans, or Puerto Ricans improved their status (Table 9.3). Again, fewer Cubans (58 percent) perceived this individual benefit from group enhancement than did Puerto Ricans (74 percent) or Mexicans (65 percent).

Respondents' opinions of the value of having Cuban, Mexican, and

Puerto Rican elected officials varied (Table 9.4). Though closely divided, more respondents agreed than disagreed that elected officials of the same national origin as the respondent helped more than other elected officials.

Questions Asked

133a, 133b, 133c, and 154.

TABLE 9.1 Should Co-Ethnics Help Each Other, by National Origin

Co-Ethnics Should Help Each Other	Mexican	Puerto Rican	Cuban
Strongly agree	206	131	38
	23.6%	22.4%	12.3%
Agree	415	295	133
	47.5%	50.3%	42.8%
Neither agree nor disagree	50	39	23
	5.8%	6.6%	7.4%
Disagree	179	109	101
	20.5%	18.5%	32.5%
Strongly disagree	23	12	16
	2.6%	2.1%	5.0%
Total	873	587	312
	100.0%	100.0%	100.0%

TABLE 9.2 Do Co-Ethnics Help or Hurt Each Other, by National Origin

Perception	Mexican	Puerto Rican	Cuban
Help each other	467	304	250
	55.0%	55.1%	82.9%
Pull each other down	382	248	52
	45.0%	44.9%	17.1%
Total	849	552	301
	100.0%	100.0%	100.0%

TABLE 9.3 Do RGs Benefit if Co-Ethnics Do Well, by National Origin

Improvement for Co-Ethnics in General Helps Respondent	*Mexican*	*Puerto Rican*	*Cuban*
Strongly agree	146	111	30
	16.8%	18.9%	9.8%
Agree	416	321	149
	47.8%	54.7%	47.8%
Neither agree nor disagree	42	39	19
	4.8%	6.6%	6.2%
Disagree	248	111	100
	28.5%	19.0%	31.9%
Strongly disagree	19	5	14
	2.2%	0.8%	4.4%
Total	871	586	312
	100.0%	100.0%	100.0%

TABLE 9.4 Level of Support from Co-Ethnic Officials, by National Origin

Co-Ethnic Officials Help More Than Non-Co-Ethnic Officials	*Mexican*	*Puerto Rican*	*Cuban*
Strongly agree	86	60	24
	9.9%	10.3%	7.7%
Agree	349	224	121
	40.1%	38.3%	39.0%
Neither agree nor disagree	76	82	34
	8.7%	14.1%	10.9%
Disagree	331	197	122
	38.0%	33.6%	39.3%
Strongly disagree	29	21	10
	3.4%	3.6%	3.2%
Total	872	585	312
	100.0%	100.0%	100.0%

B. Ethnic Organizational Behavior (Tables 9.5–9.8)

Findings

The plurality of respondents believed that there were organizations that looked out for Latino or national-origin-based interests (Table 9.5); however, few could name a specific organization that did so (Table 9.6).

The United States Hispanic Chamber of Commerce was the only organization mentioned by Mexican, Puerto Rican, and Cuban respondents. Few organizations were mentioned by members of more than one national-origin group.

Few respondents were members of or made contributions to national-origin- or Latino-based organizations (Tables 9.7 and 9.8).

Questions Asked

59a, 59b, and 59c.

TABLE 9.5 Do Latino or RG Organizations Look Out for RGs, by National Origin

Is There an Organization That Looks Out for RGs?	Mexican	Puerto Rican	Cuban
Yes	363	269	154
	41.4%	45.8%	49.5%
No	352	180	90
	40.1%	30.7%	28.9%
Don't know	162	137	68
	18.5%	23.4%	21.7%
Total	878	587	312
	100.0%	100.0%	100.0%

TABLE 9.6 Organizations That Help RGs, by National Origin (Mentioned by Ten or More Respondents)

Organization	Mexican	Puerto Rican	Cuban	Total
LULAC	98	2	0	100
Cuban American National Foundation	0	0	42	42
Asociacion Cubana America	0	0	24	24
United Farm Workers/other farmworkers' organizations	22	0	0	22
Aspira, Inc.	0	15	0	15
Institute for Puerto Rican Policy	0	15	0	15
American G.I. Forum	15	0	0	15
United States Hispanic Chamber of Commerce	11	2	1	14
National Association for Latino-Americans[a]	10	2	0	12
National Council of La Raza	12	0	0	12

[a]This organization is unknown to the authors. It could well refer to the National Association of Latino Elected Officials (NALEO).

TABLE 9.7 Membership in a Latino or RG Organization, by National Origin

Member	Mexican	Puerto Rican	Cuban
Yes	43	30	20
	4.9%	5.1%	6.4%
No	835	557	292
	95.1%	94.9%	93.6%
Total	878	587	312
	100.0%	100.0%	100.0%

TABLE 9.8   Contributions to Latino/RG Organizations, by National Origin

Contribution	Mexican	Puerto Rican	Cuban
Yes	38	21	17
	4.3%	3.6%	5.4%
No	840	566	295
	95.7%	96.4%	94.5%
Total	878	587	312
	100.0%	100.0%	100.0%

C. Ethnic Electoral Behavior (Tables 9.9–9.13)

Findings

A handful of respondents participated in political behaviors support-ing ethnic issues. Examples include signing petitions, working for a cam-paign, or writing a letter to the editor (Table 9.9).

Although Mexicans and Puerto Ricans voted at lower levels than Cu-bans, they participated at higher levels than Cubans in five of the eight nonelectoral activities we surveyed.

Few respondents had discussed national-origin-based public policy problems with others in the two weeks prior to being interviewed (Table 9.10). Cuban respondents did so at higher levels (31 percent) than either Puerto Ricans (23 percent) or Mexicans (21 percent).

Although a minority of respondents, regardless of national origin, said they were more likely to vote when a co-ethnic ran for office, large majorities indicated they did vote for the co-ethnic in an election with an Anglo opponent (Tables 9.11 and 9.13).

Among the three Latino national-origin groups, only among Cubans have the majority had the opportunity to vote for fellow Cubans (Table 9.12).

Questions Asked

88, 89, 90, 117, 127a, 127b, 127c, 127d, 127e, 127f, 127g, and 127h.

TABLE 9.9 Participation in RG Activities, by National Origin

Type of Participation	Mexican	Puerto Rican	Cuban
Volunteer campaign work for a co-ethnic	48 5.5% (n=877)	26 4.5% (n=587)	8 2.5% (n=312)
Worked to register co-ethnics to vote	72 8.2% (n=878)	35 5.9% (n=587)	14 4.4% (n=312)
Signed petition to support ethnic concerns	112 12.7% (n=878)	71 12.1% (n=585)	31 9.8% (n=312)
Attended RG meeting/demonstration	71 8.1% (n=878)	60 10.3% (n=585)	26 8.2% (n=312)
Boycotted product to support RG demand	94 10.7% (n=877)	14 2.4% (n=585)	8 2.7% (n=312)
Assisted in promoting RG culture	111 12.6% (n=878)	57 9.8% (n=585)	22 7.1% (n=312)
Wrote a letter to the editor or a public official about an RG issue	44 5.0% (n=878)	21 3.7% (n=586)	18 5.7% (n=311)
Contributed money to RG causes	75 8.6% (n=876)	43 7.3% (n=585)	31 10.1% (n=312)

TABLE 9.10 Discussion of RG Problems With Others, by National Origin

Respondent Talked to Others About RG Problems in Last Two Weeks	Mexican	Puerto Rican	Cuban
No	615 78.7%	387 76.8%	148 68.7%
Yes	167 21.3%	117 23.2%	67 31.3%
Total	782 100.0%	504 100.0%	216 100.0%

TABLE 9.11 Likelihood of Voting for Co-Ethnic, by National Origin

Likelihood of Voting for Co-Ethnic	Mexican	Puerto Rican	Cuban
More likely	198	161	58
	29.5%	37.4%	22.9%
Makes no difference	459	261	179
	68.2%	60.6%	70.4%
Less likely	16	9	17
	2.4%	2.0%	6.7%
Total	673	430	255
	100.0%	100.0%	100.0%

TABLE 9.12 Opportunity to Vote for Co-Ethnic, by National Origin

Opportunity to Vote for Co-Ethnic in the United States	Mexican	Puerto Rican	Cuban	Anglo[a]
No	511	396	141	256
	60.3%	70.2%	46.1%	67.4%
Yes	337	168	165	124
	39.7%	29.8%	53.9%	32.6%
Total	848	564	306	379
	100.0%	100.0%	100.0%	100.0%

[a]We asked Anglos about the opportunity to vote for Latinos.

TABLE 9.13 Choice in Race Between a Co-Ethnic and an Anglo, by National Origin

Choice	Mexican	Puerto Rican	Cuban	Anglo
Co-ethnic	232	126	118	44
	77.1%	79.5%	77.2%	53.4%
Anglo	37	15	23	31
	12.2%	9.3%	15.0%	38.4%
Another candidate	32	18	12	7
	10.6%	11.2%	7.8%	8.2%
Total	301	158	153	82
	100.0%	100.0%	100.0%	100.0%

D. Interest in and Knowledge of National-Origin Activities
(Tables 9.14 and 9.15)

Findings

The majority of respondents followed national-origin activities some or most of the time (Table 9.14). Puerto Ricans were more likely than either Mexicans or Cubans to follow their co-ethnics some or most of the time.

With the exception of Cubans identifying the public office held by Xavier Suarez, few respondents could identify Latino leaders (Table 9.15). Very few respondents could identify leaders who were not from their own ethnic group.

Questions Asked

126, 131c, 131d, and 131e.

TABLE 9.14 Interest in RG Activities, by National Origin

Follow RG Activities	Mexican	Puerto Rican	Cuban
Most of the time	275	273	114
	32.0%	48.1%	38.3%
Some of the time	309	161	89
	35.9%	28.5%	29.8%
Now and then	186	97	59
	21.6%	17.1%	19.8%
Hardly interested	90	36	36
	10.5%	6.3%	12.1%
Total	860	566	298
	100.0%	100.0%	100.0%

TABLE 9.15 Recognition of Latino Leaders, by National Origin

Leader (Correct or Partially Correct)	Mexican	Puerto Rican	Cuban	Anglo
Cesar Chavez	308	84	58	136
	35.2%	14.3%	18.8%	30.5%
	(n=878)	(n=587)	(n=312)	(n=446)
Robert Garcia	9	79	18	3
	0.9%	13.4%	5.7%	.8%
	(n=878)	(n=587)	(n=312)	(n=446)
Xavier Suarez	3	27	207	2
	.3%	4.6%	66.5%	.5%
	(n=878)	(n=587)	(n=312)	(n=446)

E. Public Policy Problems Facing the Latino Communities
(Tables 9.16–9.18)

Findings

The most-important problem facing each of the national-origin groups was ethnic-specific, such as the inability to work together on common problems. Cubans were more likely than Mexicans or Puerto Ricans to see ethnic-specific problems facing themselves and their co-ethnics (Table 9.16). For Mexican respondents, education was the second-most-frequently-mentioned issue. Among Puerto Ricans, social issues such as crime and drug control ranked second. Political issues such as creating a cohesive voting bloc ranked second among Cuban respondents.

All three national-origin groups saw the solution to these problems coming from government instead of individuals (Table 9.17).

By substantial majorities, Mexican and Puerto Rican respondents believed that government spending on national-origin-focused government programs should increase (Table 9.18). The majority of Cuban respondents and Anglos (asked about "Latino" programs) believed government spending in this area should stay the same.

Questions Asked

115, 116, and 125j.

TABLE 9.16 Main RG Problem, by National Origin

Main RG Problem	Mexican	Puerto Rican	Cuban
Economics	105	75	10
	14.2%	15.3%	4.8%
Social problems	86	137	17
	11.7%	27.9%	8.0%
Health care issues	4	3	0
	0.6%	0.6%	0.0%
Education	221	62	8
	29.9%	12.5%	3.8%
Immigration	21	1	2
	2.9%	0.2%	0.9%
Political issues	6	19	66
	0.8%	3.8%	30.7%
Environmental issues	4	2	2
	0.6%	0.4%	0.8%
Ethnic issues	284	178	104
	38.5%	36.2%	47.9%
Moral issues	3	6	2
	0.4%	1.1%	0.9%
Others	4	10	5
	0.5%	2.0%	2.3%
Total	739	491	216
	100.0%	100.0%	100.0%

TABLE 9.17 Role of Government Versus Individual in Solving Main RG Problem, by National Origin

Who Should Solve RG Problem	Mexican	Puerto Rican	Cuban
Individual	226	94	54
	29.1%	18.8%	24.9%
Government	550	404	162
	70.9%	81.2%	75.1%
Total	776	498	215
	100.0%	100.0%	100.0%

TABLE 9.18   Feelings About Government Spending on RG Problems,
                   by National Origin

Government Spending Should	Mexican	Puerto Rican	Cuban	Anglo[a]
Increase	607	473	120	91
	69.2%	80.8%	38.4%	20.4%
Be left the same	245	111	173	263
	27.9%	18.9%	55.6%	59.1%
Decrease	26	2	19	91
	2.9%	0.4%	6.1%	20.5%
Total	878	585	312	446
	100.0%	100.0%	100.0%	100.0%

[a]We asked Anglos about spending on Latino programs.

F. Perception of Common Ethnic Bonds Among Latinos
(Tables 9.19–9.22)

Findings

Regardless of national origin, more respondents believed that Latinos were "not very similar" culturally than believed that they were "very similar" (Table 9.19). The former constituted between 17 percent and 20 percent and the latter constituted between 22 percent for Mexicans and 35 percent for Cubans.

Few respondents believed that there were strong similarities in the political concerns of Mexicans and Puerto Ricans, Mexicans and Cubans, or Puerto Ricans and Cubans (Tables 9.20–9.22). The pairing with the highest level of "not very similar" evaluations was between Mexicans and Cubans. Forty-nine percent of Mexicans and 73 percent of Cubans felt that these groups did not have very similar political concerns.

Questions Asked

173, 174, 175, and 176.

TABLE 9.19 Belief in Common Latino Culture, by National Origin

Degree of Similarity	Mexican	Puerto Rican	Cuban
Very similar	159	117	51
	18.2%	20.0%	16.6%
Somewhat similar	522	318	149
	59.8%	54.4%	48.2%
Not very similar	193	149	109
	22.0%	25.5%	35.2%
Total	874	584	310
	100.0%	100.0%	100.0%

TABLE 9.20 Belief in Common Political Concerns of Mexicans and Puerto Ricans, by National Origin

Degree of Similarity	Mexican	Puerto Rican	Cuban
Very similar	116	46	15
	13.5%	8.3%	5.0%
Somewhat similar	387	234	98
	45.4%	41.9%	33.1%
Not very similar	350	278	182
	41.1%	49.7%	61.9%
Total	853	558	295
	100.0%	100.0%	100.0%

TABLE 9.21 Belief in Common Political Concerns of Mexicans and Cubans, by National Origin

Degree of Similarity	Mexican	Puerto Rican	Cuban
Very similar	72	46	10
	8.4%	8.3%	3.2%
Somewhat similar	362	208	71
	42.5%	37.7%	23.7%
Not very similar	418	298	219
	49.1%	54.0%	73.0%
Total	852	552	300
	100.0%	100.0%	100.0%

TABLE 9.22 Belief in Common Political Concerns of Puerto Ricans and Cubans, by National Origin

Degree of Similarity	Mexican	Puerto Rican	Cuban
Very similar	120	42	26
	14.3%	7.4%	8.7%
Somewhat similar	428	192	99
	51.0%	34.4%	32.5%
Not very similar	292	326	179
	34.8%	58.2%	58.8%
Total	839	560	304
	100.0%	100.0%	100.0%

10

The Noncitizens

The focus of this chapter is the Mexican and Cuban non-U.S. citizen respondents to the Latino National Political Survey. There are so few Puerto Rican (n = 2) and Anglo (n = 10) non-U.S. citizens that we exclude them from this analysis.

We will not repeat each table presented in the previous eight chapters of this volume. Instead, we examine the demographic characteristics of these Latino immigrants and then present a picture of key political values and attitudes. In order to allow comparison with U.S. citizen respondents, we provide the number of the table with the comparable data for the U.S. citizen population.

This chapter is divided into ten elements: (1) social and demographic characteristics; (2) citizenship and attachment to the United States; (3) psychological orientations and cultural attachment; (4) linguistic and media use patterns; (5) attachment, ideology, and governmental role; (6) attitude toward public policy issues; (7) problem solving; (8) ethnic mutual support; (9) ethnic knowledge; and (10) ethnic bonds among Latinos.

A. Social and Demographic Characteristics (Tables 10.1–10.15)

Findings

The majority of noncitizen respondents were men (Table 10.1).

Cuban and Mexican noncitizens viewed their own races differently (Table 10.2). More than nine of ten Cubans identified racially as white. More than half of Mexicans identified racially with a Latino referent; just 44 percent called themselves white.

Mexican noncitizens tended to be younger than Cuban noncitizens (Table 10.3). The modal age group for Mexicans was 25 to 34, compared to 35 to 50 for Cubans.

Almost 60 percent of each national-origin group was married (Table 10.4).

Seventy-two percent of Mexicans and 59 percent of Cubans were parents or legal guardians (Table 10.5).

Mexican immigrant households were much larger than Cuban households (Table 10.6). More than half of Mexican households had five or more members. Just 23 percent of Cuban households were comparably large.

More than 60 percent of each of these groups rented their homes (Table 10.7). Approximately one-quarter owned their homes.

Almost two-thirds of Mexicans had eight or fewer years of formal education (Table 10.8).

Three-quarters of Mexicans and 62 percent of Cubans came to the United States with eight or fewer years of education (Table 10.9).

Cuban noncitizen households had fewer members in the work force than did Mexican noncitizen households (Table 10.10).

Household income of Mexicans and Cubans was comparable (Table 10.11).

Cuban households were more likely to have earnings of between ten thousand and twenty thousand dollars per member than were Mexican households (Table 10.12)

Seventy-two percent of Mexicans and 55 percent of Cubans were in the work force (Table 10.13).

Mexicans were more likely than Cubans to be found in operator, fabricator, or laborer positions (Table 10.14). Cubans were more likely than Mexicans to be found in technical, sales, and administrative support positions.

Among the Mexicans not in the work force, almost 80 percent were homemakers (Table 10.15). Among Cubans, 36 percent were retired and 35 percent were homemakers.

Questions Asked

2, 3, 8, 9, 11, 12, 13, 24, 25b, 26a, 26b, 29, 30, 41, 180, 181, and 182.

TABLE 10.1   Gender, by National Origin, Excluding U.S. Citizens

Gender	Mexican	Cuban
Female	267	174
	40.0%	47.5%
Male	401	193
	60.0%	52.5%
Total	668	367
	100.0%	100.0%

Note: For data on U.S. citizens, see Table 3.1.

TABLE 10.2   Race, by National Origin, Excluding U.S. Citizens

Race	Mexican	Cuban
White	277	333
	44.0%	91.6%
Black	2	11
	0.3%	2.9%
Latino referent	351	20
	55.7%	5.5%
Total	630	364
	100.0%	100.0%

Note: For data on U.S. citizens, see Table 3.2.

TABLE 10.3   Age, by National Origin, Excluding U.S. Citizens

Age (years)	Mexican	Cuban
18–24	156	31
	23.4%	8.7%
25–34	248	65
	37.2%	17.9%
35–50	195	116
	29.3%	31.9%
51–65	54	84
	8.1%	23.1%
66+	13	67
	2.0%	18.4%
Total	667	363
	100.0%	100.0%

Note: For data on U.S. citizens, see Table 3.3.

TABLE 10.4   Marital Status, by National Origin, Excluding U.S. Citizens

Marital Status	Mexican	Cuban
Married	391	213
	59.3%	59.1%
Living with someone	68	12
	10.3%	3.2%
Separated or divorced	46	57
	7.0%	15.8%
Widowed	19	35
	2.9%	9.8%
Single	135	44
	20.6%	12.1%
Total	658	360
	100.0%	100.0%

Note: For data on U.S. citizens, see Table 3.4.

TABLE 10.5   Parent or Legal Guardian, by National Origin, Excluding U.S. Citizens

Respondent a Parent or Legal Guardian?	Mexican	Cuban
Yes	478	217
	71.8%	59.2%
No	187	150
	28.2%	40.8%
Total	665	367
	100.0%	100.0%

Note: For data on U.S. citizens, see Table 3.5.

TABLE 10.6   Household Size, by National Origin, Excluding U.S. Citizens

Number in Household	Mexican	Cuban
One	19	42
	2.9%	11.6%
Two	58	74
	8.7%	20.2%
Three	93	78
	13.9%	21.5%
Four	131	88
	19.7%	24.3%
Five or more	366	82
	54.9%	22.5%
Total	667	364
	100.0%	100.0%

Note: For data on U.S. citizens, see Table 3.8.

TABLE 10.7   Tenancy, by National Origin, Excluding U.S. Citizens

Tenancy	Mexican	Cuban
Rent	424	223
	63.6%	60.8%
Live with parents, who own	15	19
	2.2%	5.2%
Own	176	91
	26.4%	24.7%
Other living arrangements	52	34
	7.7%	9.3%
Total	666	367
	100.0%	100.0%

Note: For data on U.S. citizens, see Table 3.9.

TABLE 10.8   Education, by National Origin, Excluding U.S. Citizens

Education	Mexican	Cuban
0–8 years	435	164
	65.2%	45.0%
9–12 years, no degree	56	58
	8.4%	15.9%
High school diploma or GED	146	107
	21.9%	29.4%
Beyond high school	30	35
	4.6%	9.7%
Total	667	365
	100.0%	100.0%

Note: For data on U.S. citizens, see Table 3.10.

TABLE 10.9   Years of Education Completed in Country of Origin Before Emigration, by National Origin

Education in Home Country (years)	Mexican	Cuban
0–8	487	210
	75.0%	62.1%
9–12	139	93
	21.4%	27.5%
13 +	23	35
	3.5%	10.4%
Total	649	338
	100.0%	100.0%

TABLE 10.10 Household Wage Earners, by National Origin, Excluding U.S. Citizens

Salaried Workers	Mexican	Cuban
None	14 2.2%	63 17.3%
One	189 28.2%	122 33.2%
Two	222 33.3%	115 31.4%
Three	91 13.6%	42 11.3%
Four	69 10.3%	15 4.1%
Five or more	83 12.4%	10 2.7%
Total	668 100.0%	367 100.0%

Note: For data on U.S. citizens, see Table 3.11.

TABLE 10.11 Household Income, by National Origin, Excluding U.S. Citizens

Household Income	Mexican	Cuban
$0–$12,999	191 31.6%	121 38.3%
$13,000–$19,999	122 20.1%	70 22.2%
$20,000–$29,999	141 23.2%	64 20.1%
$30,000–$39,999	70 11.6%	28 8.9%
$40,000–$49,999	43 7.2%	11 3.4%
$50,000 +	39 6.4%	23 7.1%
Total	605 100.0%	317 100.0%

Note: For data on U.S. citizens, see Table 3.12.

TABLE 10.12   Per Capita Household Income, by National Origin, Excluding
U.S. Citizens

Per Capita Annual Household Income	Mexican	Cuban
$2,500 or less	153	58
	23.2%	16.6%
$2,501–$5,000	201	89
	30.6%	25.5%
$5,001–$10,000	185	112
	28.2%	31.9%
$10,001–$20,000	57	54
	8.7%	15.5%
$20,001 +	10	3
	1.5%	0.8%
Refused to answer	52	34
	7.9%	9.7%
Total	657	350
	100.0%	100.0%

Note: For data on U.S. citizens, see Table 3.13.

TABLE 10.13   Labor Force Status of Respondent, by National Origin,
Excluding U.S. Citizens

Present Work Situation of Respondent	Mexican	Cuban
In labor force	476	200
	71.5%	54.7%
Temporarily unemployed	64	28
	9.6%	7.7%
Not in labor force	126	137
	18.8%	37.5%
Total	666	366
	100.0%	100.0%

Note: For data on U.S. citizens, see Table 3.14.

TABLE 10.14   Occupation, by National Origin, Excluding U.S. Citizens

Occupation	Mexican	Cuban
Managerial, professional, or specialty	26 4.0%	17 4.5%
Technical, sales, or administrative support	36 5.6%	38 10.3%
Service	108 16.6%	48 13.0%
Farming, forestry, or fishing	100 15.3%	13 3.5%
Precision production or crafts	67 10.4%	38 10.3%
Operator, fabricator, or laborer	180 27.7%	60 16.5%
Not in labor force	134 20.5%	153 41.8%
Total	651 100.0%	366 100.0%

Note: For data on U.S. citizens, see Table 3.15.

TABLE 10.15   Reason for Not Being in the Work Force, by National Origin, Excluding U.S. Citizens

Reason for Not Being in the Labor Force	Mexican	Cuban
Unemployed	12 9.1%	19 12.2%
Disabled	3 2.2%	12 7.7%
Retired	9 6.9%	55 36.0%
Homemaker	105 78.8%	54 35.2%
Student	4 3.1%	14 8.9%
Total	134 100.0%	153 100.0%

Note: For data on U.S. citizens, see Table 3.16.

B. Citizenship and Attachment to the United States
(Tables 10.16–10.19)

Findings

The most-often cited reason given by Cubans for migrating to the United States was fleeing political problems (Table 10.16). Among Mexicans, the most-cited reason was economics.

More than 86 percent of Cubans and 76 percent of Mexicans intended to stay permanently in the United States (Table 10.17). Just 8 percent of Mexicans and 6 percent of Cubans intended to return to their home country.

Not only did Latino noncitizens want to remain in the United States, they wanted to naturalize. Fully three-quarters of Mexicans and more than 70 percent of Cubans wanted U.S. citizenship (Table 10.18). Just 17 percent of Mexicans and 24 percent of Cubans had no plans to apply for naturalization.

Almost two-thirds of Mexicans and 80 percent of Cubans emigrated to the United States as adults (Table 10.19). Despite the high levels of interest in naturalization, the process, which requires a knowledge of English, U.S. history, and civics, is often more difficult for individuals who emigrated as adults.

Questions Asked

40, 42a, 42b, 42c, 42d, 42e, 43, and 45.

TABLE 10.16   Reason for Emigration to the United States, by National Origin

Reason	*Mexican*	*Cuban*
Join family in the United States	322	175
	48.2%	47.7%
	(n=668)	(n=367)
Flee political problems	3	294
	0.4%	80.1%
	(n=668)	(n=367)
Economic reasons	494	95
	74.0%	25.9%
	(n=668)	(n=367)
Came with family	305	180
	45.7%	49.0%
	(n=668)	(n=367)
Other	88	20
	13.2%	5.4%
	(n=668)	(n=367)

TABLE 10.17   Foreign-Born Respondents' Intent to Stay in United States, by National Origin, Excluding U.S. Citizens

Respondent's Intention	Mexican	Cuban
Remain in U.S. permanently	508 76.1%	317 86.4%
Return to country of origin	56 8.4%	20 5.6%
Undecided	103 15.5%	30 8.1%
Total	668 100.0%	367 100.0%

Note: For data on all foreign-born respondents, see Table 2.33.

TABLE 10.18   Citizenship Status of Foreign-Born, by National Origin, Excluding Naturalized U.S. Citizens

U.S. Citizenship Status	Mexican	Cuban
Desires U.S. citizenship	483 76.8%	252 70.6%
Undecided	37 5.8%	18 5.2%
No plans to apply	109 17.4%	87 24.3%
Total	629 100.0%	357 100.0%

Note: For data on all foreign-born respondents, see Table 2.34.

TABLE 10.19   Age at Immigration, by National Origin, Excluding U.S. Citizens

Age at Immigration (years)	Mexican	Cuban
1–6	25 3.8%	19 5.2%
7–18	210 31.4%	56 15.3%
18+	433 64.9%	292 79.5%
Total	668 100.0%	367 100.0%

Note: For data on all foreign-born respondents, see Table 2.32.

C. Psychological Orientations and Cultural Attachment
(Tables 10.20–10.23)

Findings

Mexicans and Cubans showed low levels of trust in others (Table 10.20). Just 11 percent of Mexicans and 4 percent of Cubans believed that they could trust most people.

Higher percentages, though still a minority, believed that people try to help each other (Table 10.21). Two-thirds of Mexicans and three-quarters of Cubans believed that "others look out for themselves."

Latino immigrant noncitizens were evenly divided over whether people's lives are determined from within or without (Table 10.22). Fifty-five percent of Mexicans and 50 percent of Cubans believed that lives were determined by outsiders.

The relationship of hard work to success is also in doubt in this population. Fifty-eight percent of Mexicans and 54 percent of Cubans agreed with the statement that hard work leads to success.

There was almost universal support for equal opportunity.

Approximately 60 percent of Latino immigrants accepted that there would be inequality as a function of chance.

Overwhelming majorities of Mexicans and Cubans identified themselves using national-origin-based terms (Table 10.23). Just 12 percent of Mexicans and 9 percent of Cubans preferred pan-ethnic identifications such as Latino or Hispanic. Few preferred to use the term "American."

Questions Asked

5, 141a, 141b, 152, 153, 156a, and 156b.

TABLE 10.20   Trust of Others, by National Origin, Excluding U.S. Citizens

Degree of Trust	*Mexican*	*Cuban*
Trust most people	76	13
	11.4%	3.5%
Must be careful with most people	592	354
	88.6%	96.5%
Total	668	367
	100.0%	100.0%

Note: For data on U.S. citizens, see Table 4.1.

TABLE 10.21 Belief in Helpfulness of People, by National Origin, Excluding U.S. Citizens

Degree of Helpfulness	Mexican	Cuban
People try to help each other	209	89
	31.8%	24.3%
Others look out for themselves	448	276
	68.2%	75.7%
Total	656	365
	100.0%	100.0%

Note: For data on U.S. citizens, see Table 4.2.

TABLE 10.22 Who or What Determines Success and Opportunity, by National Origin, Excluding U.S. Citizens

Belief	Mexican	Cuban
Success determined by outsiders	334	164
	55.2%	49.9%
	(n=605)	(n=328)
Hard work leads to success	365	177
	57.8%	54.1%
	(n=633)	(n=327)
Society should promote equal opportunity	629	350
	97.0%	98.7%
	(n=648)	(n=355)
Inequality by chance is acceptable	398	206
	63.3%	59.3%
	(n=630)	(n=347)

Note: For data on U.S. citizens, see Table 4.3.

TABLE 10.23   Preferred Ethnic Identification, by National Origin,
                Excluding U.S. Citizens

Ethnic Identification	Mexican	Cuban
Mexican origin	576	0
	87.7%	0.0%
Cuban origin	0	319
	0.0%	88.5%
Pan-ethnic	78	32
	12.0%	8.8%
American	2	10
	0.3%	2.7%
Total	657	361
	100.0%	100.0%

Notes: For data on U.S. citizens, see Table 4.6.

The preferred identification terms among Mexican respondents are Mexican (47), Mexicano(a) (508), Mexican-American (21), Hispanic (20), Latino(a) (25), Spanish (10), Spanish American (3), Hispano (20), and American (2).

Among Cuban respondents, the preferred terms are Cuban (319), Hispanic (6), Latino(a) (8), Spanish (2), Spanish American (5), Hispano (10), and American (10).

D. Linguistic and Media Use Patterns (Tables 10.24 to 10.30)

Findings

Approximately 86 percent of Cuban and Mexican noncitizens used Spanish, either exclusively or dominantly (Table 10.24). Just 6 percent of Mexicans and 4 percent of Cubans reported that they were more likely to use English than Spanish.

Among noncitizens who chose to be interviewed in English, few were functional in Spanish (Table 10.25). These English-dominant noncitizen respondents may have emigrated as children and had little experience or reinforcement in Spanish.

The majority of respondents who answered the LNPS questions in Spanish were literate in English (Table 10.26).

Television was the most-used media for news (Table 10.27).

Approximately 61 percent of Cubans and 57 percent of Mexicans who were not U.S. citizens relied exclusively on Spanish-language media for news (Table 10.28). Slightly more than one-quarter of the noncitizen respondents used a combination of Spanish and English media.

Majorities in both the Mexican and the Cuban noncitizen communities did not rely on the newspaper for news (Table 10.29).

Three-quarters of Cubans and one-half of Mexicans watched television for news four to seven days per week (Table 10.30).

Questions Asked

48, 49, 51, 52, 53, 168, and SAQ2.

TABLE 10.24   Home Language of Respondent, by National Origin, Excluding U.S. Citizens

Language Spoken in the Home	Mexican	Cuban
Only Spanish	384 57.5%	224 61.3%
More Spanish than English	187 28.0%	90 24.6%
Both languages	60 9.0%	36 9.9%
More English than Spanish	23 3.4%	3 0.9%
Only English	14 2.1%	12 3.4%
Total	667 100.0%	365 100.0%

Note: For data on U.S. citizens, see Table 4.9.

TABLE 10.25   Spanish Literacy of Respondents Interviewed in English, by National Origin, Excluding U.S. Citizens

Spanish Literacy of the English-Dominant	Mexican	Cuban
Low	63 86.3%	41 84.5%
High	10 13.7%	7 15.5%
Total	73 100.0%	48 100.0%

Note: For data on U.S. citizens, see Table 4.11.

TABLE 10.26   English Literacy of Respondents Interviewed in Spanish, by National Origin, Excluding U.S. Citizens

English Literacy of the Spanish-Dominant	Mexican	Cuban
Low	215	81
	36.2%	25.5%
High	379	237
	63.8%	74.5%
Total	594	318
	100.0%	100.0%

Note: For data on U.S. citizens, see Table 4.10.

TABLE 10.27   Most-Used News Source, by National Origin, Excluding U.S. Citizens

Most-Used News Source	Mexican	Cuban
Television	560	301
	84.2%	83.5%
Newspapers	42	23
	6.4%	6.4%
Magazines	2	1
	0.3%	0.4%
Radio	61	35
	9.2%	9.7%
Total	665	361
	100.0%	100.0%

Note: For data on U.S. citizens, see Table 5.1.

TABLE 10.28   Language of Two Most-Used News Sources, by National Origin, Excluding U.S. Citizens

Language of News Sources	Mexican	Cuban
English	86	45
	13.6%	13.0%
Both English and Spanish	184	92
	29.1%	26.4%
Spanish	363	210
	57.3%	60.6%
Total	633	346
	100.0%	100.0%

Note: For data on U.S. citizens, see Table 5.2.

TABLE 10.29   Newspaper Readership, by National Origin,
                   Excluding U.S. Citizens

Frequency of Newspaper Readership for Political News During the Week Preceding the LNPS Interview	*Mexican*	*Cuban*
Don't read newspaper	3	6
	0.5%	1.6%
0 days	399	176
	59.9%	47.9%
1–3 days	155	72
	23.2%	19.7%
4–7 days	109	113
	16.4%	30.8%
Total	667	366
	100.0%	100.0%

Note: For data on U.S. citizens, see Table 5.3.

TABLE 10.30   Television Viewership for News, by National Origin,
                   Excluding U.S. Citizens

Frequency of Watching Television News During the Week Preceding the LNPS Interview	*Mexican*	*Cuban*
Don't watch television news	3	6
	0.5%	1.6%
0 days	106	25
	15.9%	6.7%
1–3 days	225	58
	33.7%	15.7%
4–7 days	333	278
	49.9%	76.0%
Total	667	366
	100.0%	100.0%

Note: For data on U.S. citizens, see Table 5.4.

E. Attachment, Ideology, and Government Role (Tables 10.31–10.39)

Findings

Seventy-six percent of Cuban and 61 percent of Mexican noncitizens felt either very strong or extremely strong attachment to the United States (Table 10.31).

The majority of Cubans and Mexicans trusted the government most or all of the time (Table 10.32). Just 8 percent of Mexicans and 4 percent of Cubans never trusted the government.

This strong attachment to the United States and trust in government is reflected in the fact that more than 80 percent of Cuban and Mexican noncitizens believed that government was run for the benefit of all (Table 10.33).

Mexican and Cuban noncitizens were more likely to identify themselves as conservative than liberal (Table 10.34). Among Cubans, 49 percent identified themselves as conservative; the rate for Mexicans was 44 percent.

Although slightly more likely among Mexicans than Cubans, both national-origin groups were more likely to believe that government should provide jobs than they were to believe that individuals should provide jobs (Table 10.35). Just one-fifth of noncitizen respondents expressed neutrality on this question.

Latino noncitizen immigrants were also more likely to believe that government, not individuals, should provide housing (Table 10.36).

The locus for providing a minimum income rested more with the individual than with the government (Table 10.37). Forty-four percent of Mexicans and 40 percent of Cubans felt that individuals should provide their own minimum income.

Social problems topped the list of problems facing the nation and the respondents' cities (Tables 10.38 and 10.39). Economic issues were second.

Questions Asked

46, 107, 108, 109, 111, 128, 129, 130, and 142.

TABLE 10.31   Love for the United States, by National Origin, Excluding U.S. Citizens

Strength of Love for U.S.	Mexican	Cuban
Extremely strong	81	131
	12.2%	35.9%
Very strong	325	147
	48.9%	40.3%
Somewhat strong	174	72
	26.2%	19.7%
Not very strong	84	15
	12.6%	4.1%
Total	665	365
	100.0%	100.0%

Note: For data on U.S. citizens, see Table 6.1.

TABLE 10.32   Trust, by National Origin, Excluding U.S. Citizens

Degree of Trust in Government Officials to Do What Is Right	Mexican	. Cuban
Just about always	181	142
	27.4%	38.9%
Most of the time	180	103
	27.3%	28.1%
Some of the time	245	105
	37.2%	28.7%
Almost never	53	16
	8.1%	4.2%
Total	659	366
	100.0%	100.0%

Note: For data on U.S. citizens, see Table 6.3.

TABLE 10.33   Whom Government Serves, by National Origin, Excluding U.S. Citizens

Government Is Run	Mexican	Cuban
By the few in their interest	106	51
	16.5%	14.6%
For the benefit of all	536	299
	83.5%	85.4%
Total	641	350
	100.0%	100.0%

Note: For data on U.S. citizens, see Table 6.4.

TABLE 10.34   Ideology, by National Origin, Excluding U.S. Citizens

Ideology	Mexican	Cuban
Very liberal	12	16
	1.8%	4.5%
Liberal	102	58
	15.6%	16.3%
Slightly liberal	79	21
	12.2%	6.0%
Moderate	175	85
	26.9%	24.2%
Slightly conservative	124	57
	19.1%	16.2%
Conservative	124	91
	19.1%	25.8%
Very conservative	35	25
	5.4%	7.0%
Total	651	352
	100.0%	100.0%

Notes: For data on U.S. citizens, see Table 6.7.

TABLE 10.35   Government versus Individual Role in Job Provision, by National Origin, Excluding U.S. Citizens

Who Should Provide Jobs?	Mexican	Cuban
Government should provide a job for everyone who needs one		
1	275	120
	41.1%	32.6%
2	39	27
	5.8%	7.3%
3	137	84
	20.4%	22.8%
4	42	22
	6.2%	6.0%
5	177	115
Individuals should get their own	26.4%	31.4%
Total	668	367
	100.0%	100.0%

Notes: For data on U.S. citizens, see Table 6.9.

Respondents were asked to place themselves on a scale of one to five between the extreme positions indicated.

TABLE 10.36   Government versus Individual Role in Housing Provision, by National Origin, Excluding U.S. Citizens

Who Should Provide Housing?	Mexican	Cuban
Government should provide to people who need		
1	242	125
	36.3%	34.0%
2	50	25
	7.5%	6.7%
3	157	109
	23.5%	29.7%
4	29	23
	4.4%	6.1%
5	189	86
Individual should provide	28.3%	23.5%
Total	667	366
	100.0%	100.0%

Notes: For data on U.S. citizens, see Table 6.10.

Respondents were asked to place themselves on a scale of one to five between the extreme positions indicated.

TABLE 10.37   Government versus Individual Role in Assuring Minimum Income, by National Origin, Excluding U.S. Citizens

Who Should Provide a Minimum Income?	Mexican	Cuban
Government should provide, if needed		
1	155	75
	23.3%	20.4%
2	48	32
	7.2%	8.8%
3	174	111
	26.1%	30.4%
4	38	35
	5.7%	9.6%
5	252	113
Individual should provide	37.8%	30.8%
Total	667	367
	100.0%	100.0%

Notes: For data on U.S. citizens, see Table 6.11.

Respondents were asked to place themselves on a scale of one to five between the extreme positions indicated.

TABLE 10.38   Most-Important National Problem, by National Origin,
Excluding U.S. Citizens

Principal National Problem	Mexican	Cuban
Economics	97	44
	16.6%	13.2%
Social problems	371	231
	63.7%	69.2%
Health care issues	14	7
	2.4%	2.0%
Education	31	6
	5.3%	1.9%
Immigration	10	5
	1.7%	1.6%
Political issues	24	27
	4.1%	8.0%
Environment issues	3	2
	0.5%	0.7%
Ethnic issues	22	8
	3.8%	2.3%
Moral issues	2	2
	0.3%	0.5%
Others	9	2
	1.6%	0.7%
Total	582	333
	100.0%	100.0%

Note: For data on U.S. citizens, see Table 7.1.

TABLE 10.39 Most-Important Local Problem, by National Origin, Excluding U.S. Citizens

Principal Local Problem	Mexican	Cuban
Economics	80	34
	16.3%	11.2%
Social problems	301	229
	61.2%	74.6%
Health care issues	8	2
	1.7%	0.7%
Education	26	2
	5.2%	0.5%
Immigration	1	4
	0.2%	1.3%
Political issues	23	8
	4.7%	2.7%
Environmental issues	23	3
	4.6%	1.0%
Ethnic issues	21	13
	4.2%	4.4%
Moral issues	5	1
	0.9%	0.5%
Others	4	10
	0.9%	3.2%
Total	492	307
	100.0%	100.0%

Note: For data on U.S. citizens, see Table 7.2.

F. Attitude Toward Public Policy Issues (Tables 10.40–10.69)

Findings

Across a broad range of domestic policy issues, noncitizen Mexicans and Cubans saw a need for increased government spending, even if it required that they pay more taxes (Table 10.40). The three issues that received the highest levels of support for added spending were crime and drugs, education, and health. Mexicans were more likely than Cubans to call for added government spending in eight of the ten public policy areas we surveyed.

One-quarter of Mexicans and 11 percent of Cubans perceived that they had been discriminated against because of their national origin (Table 10.41).

Fewer than 10 percent reported that they had faced discrimination on the part of a public official (Table 10.42). This pattern remains true, regardless of the ethnicity of the public official (Table 10.43).

Noncitizen Latinos did not perceive that society discriminated a great deal against racial, ethnic, gender, or religious groups (Tables 10.44–10.50). When asked about discrimination against African Americans, Asian Americans, Mexican Americans, Cuban Americans, Puerto Ricans, women, and Jewish Americans, more than 20 percent of the respondents reported that just two groups—African Americans and Mexican Americans—faced "a lot" of discrimination.

While the majority opposed making English the official language of the United States, sizable minorities supported this proposition (Table 10.51).

More than 95 percent of each of these populations believed that public services should be provided in Spanish (Table 10.52). Eighty-four percent of Cubans and 68 percent of Mexicans opposed the proposition that businesses could require that their employees use English (Table 10.53).

These populations believed that U.S. citizens should learn English (Table 10.54). As majorities of these populations desired to naturalize as U.S. citizens (Table 10.18), this finding suggests a commitment to learn English.

Cubans and Mexicans disagreed over the proposition that preference should be given to immigrants from Latin American (Table 10.55). Almost three-quarters of Mexican noncitizens supported the proposition. The majority of Cubans opposed the notion.

Despite their own immigrant status, more than 83 percent of Mexicans and 72 percent of Cubans believed that there were too many immigrants coming to the United States (Table 10.56).

These noncitizens disagreed with the assertion that U.S. citizens should be hired over noncitizens (Table 10.57). Interestingly, 31 percent of Mexicans and 36 percent of Cubans agreed that citizens should be hired before noncitizens.

Fifty-two percent of Cubans and 38 percent of Mexicans were more concerned about U.S. issues than about issues in the home country (Table 10.58). Just 20 percent of Mexicans and 14 percent of Cubans focused more on issues in their country of origin.

Nearly two-thirds of Cuban noncitizens opposed establishing diplomatic relations with Cuba (Table 10.59). A somewhat smaller majority of Mexicans (55 percent) supported U.S.-Cuban diplomatic relations.

One-fifth of respondents believed that Puerto Rico should become a state (Table 10.60). The option receiving the greatest support was Commonwealth status. More than two-thirds of Mexican and Cuban advocated this option.

More than 80 percent of Mexicans and 90 percent of Cubans attributed Mexico's problems to internal corruption (Table 10.61). Few blamed U.S. policy.

Eighty percent of Cubans believed that the United States should be more involved in Central America (Table 10.62). Almost 60 percent of Mexicans, on the other hand, believed that the United States should be less involved.

Almost two-thirds of Mexicans attributed Central America's problems to poverty and the lack of human rights (Table 10.63). Half of the Cuban respondents blamed Cuban, Soviet, and Nicaraguan interference.

Mexican and Cuban respondents were more likely to believe that women were better off if they had careers and jobs than if they stayed home and reared children (Table 10.64).

Approximately one-half of respondents believed that men and women were equally capable of holding public office (Table 10.65). Among those believing that one of the sexes is more capable than the other in public office, those choosing men were more common than those choosing women.

Mexicans and Cubans had different opinions as to who should care for the household and children (Table 10.66). Fifty-eight percent of Cubans and 44 percent of Mexicans believed that men and women should care for children equally. Among those who believed that one of the sexes should have more responsibility, Mexicans were more likely than Cubans to indicate that men should have the greater responsibility.

The majority of respondents, regardless of national origin, opposed abortion under most circumstances (Table 10.67). One-third of Cubans and 17 percent of Mexicans would allow it under any circumstances.

The Mexican non-U.S. citizen community was evenly divided on the question of the appropriateness of college admission quotas (Table 10.68). Slightly more than one-third were neutral, one-third opposed quotas, and one-third favored them. Almost half of Cubans favored college admission based strictly on merit.

Almost two-thirds of Cubans and 43 percent of Mexicans favored capital punishment (Table 10.69). Just 28 percent of Mexicans and 17 percent of Cubans opposed it.

Questions Asked

69, 70, 71, 125a, 125b, 125c, 125d, 125e, 125f, 125g, 125h, 125i, 125j, 125k, 134, 135, 136, 137, 147, 148, 149, 150a, 150b, 150c, 150d, 150e, 150f, 150g, 151, 155, 157, 158, 159, 160, 161a, 161b, 161c, 161d, 167a, 167b, and 167c.

TABLE 10.40   Attitude Toward Government Spending on Public Policy Areas, by National Origin, Excluding U.S. Citizens

Government Spending Should Increase on	Mexican	Cuban
Crime and drugs	581 87.2% (n=666)	330 89.9% (n=367)
Education	560 83.8% (n=668)	285 77.7% (n=367)
Health	544 82.0% (n=664)	269 73.4% (n=367)
Child services	507 76.2% (n=666)	251 68.5% (n=366)
Environment	418 62.8% (n=666)	221 60.1% (n=367)
Welfare	258 38.8% (n=665)	145 39.7% (n=365)
Science and technology	413 61.9% (n=666)	207 56.5% (n=366)
Defense	235 35.4% (n=665)	130 35.5% (n=367)
Black issues	436 65.5% (n=666)	184 50.2% (n=367)
Refugee/immigrant services	536 80.6% (n=665)	245 66.8% (n=366)

Note: For data on U.S. citizens, see Tables 7.3 and 7.4.

TABLE 10.41 Personal Experience With Discrimination, by National Origin, Excluding U.S. Citizens

Respondent Discriminated Against Because of National Origin	*Mexican*	*Cuban*
Yes	176	40
	26.3%	10.8%
No	492	327
	73.7%	89.2%
Total	668	367
	100.0%	100.0%

Note: For data on U.S. citizens, see Table 7.5.

TABLE 10.42 Experiences With Public Officials, by National Origin, Excluding U.S. Citizens

Treatment by a Public Official	*Mexican*	*Cuban*
Treated as well as anyone else	180	80
	91.3%	96.0%
Others treated better	17	3
	8.7%	4.0%
Total	197	83
	100.0%	100.0%

Note: For data on U.S. citizens, see Table 7.6.

TABLE 10.43   Differences in Treatment by Anglo and Co-Ethnic Public
Officials, by National Origin, Excluding U.S. Citizens

Treatment by Officials	Mexican	Cuban
Treatment by Anglo Officials		
Provided equal treatment	106	49
	91.4%	96.1%
Treated others better	10	2
	8.6%	3.9%
Total	116	51
	100.0%	100.0%
Treatment by RG Officials		
Provided equal treatment	73	30
	92.4%	96.8%
Treated others better	6	1
	7.6%	3.2%
Total	79	31
	100.0%	100.0%

Note: For data on U.S. citizens, see Table 7.7.

TABLE 10.44   Perception of Discrimination Against African Americans, by
National Origin, Excluding U.S. Citizens

Degree of Discrimination Against Blacks	Mexican	Cuban
A lot	213	75
	32.3%	20.6%
Some	249	109
	37.8%	29.7%
A little	118	56
	17.9%	15.2%
None	79	126
	12.1%	34.5%
Total	659	366
	100.0%	100.0%

Note: For data on U.S. citizens, see Table 7.8.

TABLE 10.45   Perception of Discrimination Against Asian Americans, by National Origin, Excluding U.S. Citizens

Degree of Discrimination Against Asians	Mexican	Cuban
A lot	34	14
	5.3%	3.9%
Some	165	89
	25.4%	25.2%
A little	234	57
	36.1%	16.1%
None	215	195
	33.1%	54.9%
Total	647	355
	100.0%	100.0%

Note: For data on U.S. citizens, see Table 7.9

TABLE 10.46   Perception of Discrimination Against Mexican Americans, by National Origin, Excluding U.S. Citizens

Degree of Discrimination Against Mexican Americans	Mexican	Cuban
A lot	207	73
	31.1%	20.5%
Some	238	93
	35.8%	25.9%
A little	165	63
	24.8%	17.7%
None	56	128
	8.4%	35.9%
Total	666	357
	100.0%	100.0%

Note: For data on U.S. citizens, see Table 7.10.

TABLE 10.47　　Perception of Discrimination Against Cuban Americans,
　　　　　　　　　　by National Origin, Excluding U.S. Citizens

Degree of Discrimination Against Cuban Americans	*Mexican*	*Cuban*
A lot	63	26
	10.1%	7.0%
Some	219	99
	34.9%	27.1%
A little	211	50
	33.6%	13.6%
None	134	191
	21.4%	52.2%
Total	627	365
	100.0%	100.0%

Note: For data on U.S. citizens, see Table 7.11.

TABLE 10.48　　Perception of Discrimination Against Puerto Ricans,
　　　　　　　　　　by National Origin, Excluding U.S. Citizens

Degree of Discrimination Against Puerto Ricans	*Mexican*	*Cuban*
A lot	40	22
	6.3%	6.0%
Some	178	101
	28.1%	28.0%
A little	215	41
	33.8%	11.2%
None	202	198
	31.8%	54.7%
Total	634	362
	100.0%	100.0%

Note: For data on U.S. citizens, see Table 7.12.

TABLE 10.49 Perception of Discrimination Against Women, by National Origin, Excluding U.S. Citizens

Degree of Discrimination Against Women	Mexican	Cuban
A lot	77	15
	11.9%	4.3%
Some	162	81
	25.1%	22.6%
A little	188	56
	29.1%	15.6%
None	220	205
	34.0%	57.5%
Total	647	358
	100.0%	100.0%

Note: For data on U.S. citizens, see Table 7.13.

TABLE 10.50 Perception of Discrimination Against Jewish Americans, by National Origin, Excluding U.S. Citizens

Degree of Discrimination Against Jewish Americans	Mexican	Cuban
A lot	48	6
	7.9%	1.7%
Some	139	46
	22.7%	13.1%
A little	176	44
	28.7%	12.3%
None	250	257
	40.8%	72.8%
Total	612	353
	100.0%	100.0%

Note: For data on U.S. citizens, see Table 7.14.

TABLE 10.51   English as the Official Language, by National Origin, Excluding U.S. Citizens

English Should Be the Official Language	Mexican	Cuban
Strongly agree	52 8.4%	26 7.3%
Agree	210 33.7%	94 26.8%
Disagree	296 47.4%	161 45.7%
Strongly disagree	66 10.5%	71 20.1%
Total	624 100.0%	351 100.0%

Note: For data on U.S. citizens, see Table 7.15.

TABLE 10.52   Attitude Toward Public Service Provision in Spanish, by National Origin, Excluding U.S. Citizens

Public Services Should Be Provided In Spanish	Mexican	Cuban
Strongly agree	196 29.9%	145 40.5%
Agree	435 66.3%	199 55.5%
Disagree	24 3.6%	14 3.9%
Strongly disagree	2 0.3%	0 0.1%
Total	657 100.0%	358 100.0%

Note: For data on U.S. citizens, see Table 7.16.

TABLE 10.53 Attitudes Toward Requiring the Use of English in the Work Place, by National Origin, Excluding U.S. Citizens

Businesses Can Require the Use of English During Working Hours	Mexican	Cuban
Strongly agree	47 7.2%	1 0.4%
Agree	158 24.4%	52 15.1%
Disagree	371 57.3%	209 60.6%
Strongly disagree	72 11.1%	82 23.8%
Total	648 100.0%	344 100.0%

Note: For data on U.S. citizens, see Table 7.17.

TABLE 10.54 U.S. Citizens and Residents Should Learn English, by National Origin, Excluding U.S. Citizens

Citizens and Residents of the U.S. Should Learn English	Mexican	Cuban
Strongly agree	155 23.6%	70 19.9%
Agree	459 69.9%	251 71.8%
Disagree	35 5.3%	22 6.3%
Strongly disagree	8 1.2%	7 2.0%
Total	657 100.0%	350 100.0%

Note: For data on U.S. citizens, see Table 7.18.

TABLE 10.55   Preference for Latin American Immigration, by National Origin, Excluding U.S. Citizens

Preference Should be Given to Latin American Immigrants	Mexican	Cuban
Strongly agree	103	22
	16.7%	6.9%
Agree	353	129
	57.3%	41.0%
Disagree	156	129
	25.3%	41.2%
Strongly disagree	4	34
	0.7%	10.8%
Total	615	314
	100.0%	100.0%

Note: For data on U.S. citizens, see Table 7.23.

TABLE 10.56   Attitude Toward Volume of Current Immigration, by National Origin, Excluding U.S. Citizens

There Are Too Many Immigrants	Mexican	Cuban
Strongly agree	105	51
	17.3%	15.0%
Agree	401	195
	66.3%	57.7%
Disagree	96	79
	15.9%	23.2%
Strongly disagree	3	14
	0.5%	4.0%
Total	604	339
	100.0%	100.0%

Note: For data on U.S. citizens, see Table 7.24.

TABLE 10.57   Attitude Toward Job Preference for Citizens, by National Origin, Excluding U.S. Citizens

U.S. Citizens Should Be Hired Over Noncitizens	Mexican	Cuban
Strongly agree	20	19
	3.2%	5.9%
Agree	178	96
	28.8%	30.3%
Disagree	360	153
	58.4%	48.1%
Strongly disagree	59	50
	9.6%	15.7%
Total	617	318
	100.0%	100.0%

Note: For data on U.S. citizens, see Table 7.25.

TABLE 10.58   Concern with U.S. or Homeland Politics, by National Origin, Excluding U.S. Citizens

Focus of Concern	Mexican	Cuban
More with homeland	124	48
	20.4%	14.2%
U.S. and homeland equally	255	115
	42.0%	34.2%
More with U.S.	228	174
	37.6%	51.6%
Total	608	336
	100.0%	100.0%

Note: For data on U.S. citizens, see Table 7.26.

TABLE 10.59   U.S. Establishment of Diplomatic Relations With Cuba, by
                  National Origin, Excluding U.S. Citizens

Should U.S. Establish Relations With Cuba?	Mexican	Cuban
No	231	219
	44.6%	65.5%
Yes	287	115
	55.4%	34.5%
Total	518	334
	100.0%	100.0%

Note: For data on U.S. citizens, see Table 7.27.

TABLE 10.60   Attitude Toward the Status of Puerto Rico, by National Origin,
                  Excluding U.S. Citizens

Preferred Status of Puerto Rico	Mexican	Cuban
A state	108	62
	20.2%	22.2%
A Commonwealth	358	196
	67.2%	69.6%
Independent	67	23
	12.7%	8.2%
Total	533	282
	100.0%	100.0%

Note: For data on U.S. citizens, see Table 7.28.

TABLE 10.61   Causes of Problems in Mexico, by National Origin,
                  Excluding U.S. Citizens

Cause of Problems in Mexico	Mexican	Cuban
U.S. policy	42	11
	6.7%	3.8%
U.S. policy and corruption in Mexico	65	7
	10.3%	2.5%
Mexican corruption	523	279
	82.8%	93.5%
Total	632	298
	100.0%	100.0%

Note: For data on U.S. citizens, see Table 7.29.

TABLE 10.62 Attitude Toward U.S. Involvement in Central America, by National Origin, Excluding U.S. Citizens

Level of U.S. Involvement in Central America	Mexican	Cuban
Should be more involved	258	279
	40.9%	79.7%
Should be less involved	374	71
	59.1%	20.3%
Total	632	349
	100.0%	100.0%

Note: For data on U.S. citizens, see Table 7.30.

TABLE 10.63 Cause of Unrest in Central America, by National Origin, Excluding U.S. Citizens

Cause of Unrest in Central America	Mexican	Cuban
Cuban interference	127	181
	19.7%	50.5%
Cuban interference and poverty/ lack of human rights	96	86
	14.9%	24.0%
Poverty/lack of human rights	421	91
	65.5%	25.4%
Total	643	358
	100.0%	100.0%

Note: For data on U.S. citizens, see Table 7.31.

TABLE 10.64   Role of Women, by National Origin, Excluding U.S. Citizens

Should Women Be in the Home or Have Careers?	Mexican		Cuban	
	Female	*Male*	*Female*	*Male*
Women better off if they stay home and rear children				
1	58	93	42	49
	21.8%	23.3%	24.5%	25.5%
2	14	12	14	4
	5.1%	3.0%	7.8%	1.9%
3	82	96	49	41
	30.6%	23.9%	28.5%	21.5%
4	21	13	9	13
	7.8%	3.3%	5.1%	6.7%
5	93	186	59	85
Women better off if they have careers and jobs	34.6%	46.5%	34.1%	44.5%
Total	267	401	173	192
	100.0%	100.0%	100.0%	100.0%

Notes: For data on U.S. citizens, see Table 7.33.

Respondents were asked to place themselves on a scale of one to five between the extreme positions indicated.

TABLE 10.65 Attitude Toward Women in Public Office During Crises, by National Origin, Excluding U.S. Citizens

Women's Capability in Office During Crisis	Mexican		Cuban	
	Female	*Male*	*Female*	*Male*
Men more capable than women in public office during crisis				
1	65	135	31	57
	24.2%	33.8%	18.1%	29.5%
2	10	22	13	13
	3.6%	5.4%	7.5%	7.0%
3	138	184	106	99
	51.7%	46.2%	61.1%	51.6%
4	12	14	5	3
	4.6%	3.4%	3.1%	1.7%
5	42	44	18	19
Women more capable than men in public office during crisis	15.9%	11.1%	10.1%	10.1%
Total	266	399	173	192
	100.0%	100.0%	100.0%	100.0%

Notes: For data on U.S. citizens, see Table 7.34.

Respondents were asked to place themselves on a scale of one to five between the extreme positions indicated.

TABLE 10.66 Responsibility for Home and Children, by National Origin, Excluding U.S. Citizens

	Mexican		Cuban	
Primary Caregiver	*Female*	*Male*	*Female*	*Male*
Even if it limits career, women should care for home and children				
1.	36	73	23	41
	13.6%	18.3%	13.5%	21.4%
2.	12	29	7	12
	4.5%	7.3%	3.9%	6.3%
3.	125	170	100	109
	46.7%	42.7%	59.1%	57.0%
4.	14	9	16	2
	5.1%	2.3%	9.2%	.9%
5.	80	117	24	28
Even if it limits career, men should care for home and children	30.1%	29.3%	14.2%	14.4%
Total	267	399	169	192
	100.0%	100.0%	100.0%	100.0%

Notes: For data on U.S. citizens, see Table 7.35.

Respondents were asked to place themselves on a scale of one to five between the extreme positions indicated.

TABLE 10.67 Attitude Toward Abortion, by National Origin, Excluding U.S. Citizens

Conditions Under Which Abortion Should Be Permitted	Mexican		Cuban	
	Female	*Male*	*Female*	*Male*
None	70	116	25	40
	26.0%	29.2%	14.5%	20.5%
Rape/incest	110	156	55	56
	41.3%	39.5%	31.5%	29.0%
Only if needed	35	62	43	29
	13.2%	15.8%	24.8%	15.2%
Any	52	61	51	68
	19.5%	15.5%	29.2%	35.3%
Total	267	395	174	193
	100.0%	100.0%	100.0%	100.0%

Note: For data on U.S. citizens, see Table 7.38.

TABLE 10.68   Job and College Admission Quotas, by National Origin, Excluding U.S. Citizens

Basis of Jobs and College Admission	Mexican	Cuban
Government quotas		
1	177	60
	27.5%	16.8%
2	34	24
	5.3%	6.8%
3	223	97
	34.7%	27.1%
4	36	27
	5.6%	7.5%
5	173	150
Strictly merit	26.9%	41.8%
Total	643	358
	100.0%	100.0%

Notes: For data on U.S. citizens, see Table 7.36.

Respondents were asked to place themselves on a scale of one to five between the extreme positions indicated.

TABLE 10.69   Attitude Toward Capital Punishment, by National Origin, Excluding U.S. Citizens

Opinion of Capital Punishment for Convicted Murderers	Mexican	Cuban
Support	282	233
	43.3%	63.6%
Depends on the case	187	71
	28.7%	19.4%
Oppose	182	62
	28.0%	17.1%
Total	651	366
	100.0%	100.0%

Note: For data on U.S. citizens, see Table 7.37.

G. Problem Solving (Tables 10.70–10.73)

Findings

In the twelve months prior to being interviewed, more than 70 percent of noncitizen respondents had not contacted a government office (Table 10.70). Among those who had contacted government offices, the most frequent reason was to obtain services.

Few respondents identified specific local problems (Table 10.71). Among those who did, the majority identified social problems. The most common strategy used to address these local problems was collective action (Table 10.72).

The respondents were more likely to participate in problem-solving strategies surrounding the schools than they were to address local problems (Table 10.73). More than half of respondents who had children had met with a teacher. More than 40 percent had attended PTA meetings or met with the school principal. Surprisingly, considering that these respondents were not United States citizens, 29 percent of Mexicans and 23 percent of Cubans reported that had voted in school board elections.

Questions Asked

65, 66, 106a, 106b, 106c, 106d, 106e, 119, 120, 121, and 122.

TABLE 10.70   Reasons for Visiting Government Office, by National Origin, Excluding U.S. Citizens

Reason for Government Contact During Twelve Months Before Interview	Mexican	Cuban
Clarify regulations	42 7.9%	27 8.7%
Immigration	4 0.8%	3 1.0%
Services	62 11.7%	42 13.6%
Employment	11 2.1%	5 1.6%
Other	20 3.8%	14 4.5%
No government contacts	391 73.8%	218 70.6%
Total	530 100.0%	309 100.0%

Note: For data on U.S. citizens, see Table 8.5.

TABLE 10.71 Cooperative Efforts at Problem Solving, by National Origin, Excluding U.S. Citizens

Problem Type	Mexican	Cuban
Economic	5	3
	0.9%	1.0%
Social	53	28
	10.0%	9.0%
Health	5	2
	0.9%	0.6%
Education	7	1
	1.3%	0.3%
Political	11	7
	2.1%	2.2%
Environment	9	7
	1.7%	2.2%
Ethnic	2	1
	0.4%	0.3%
Moral	1	2
	0.2%	0.6%
Other	5	0
	0.9%	0.0%
None	430	261
	81.4%	83.7%
Total	528	312
	100.0%	100.0%

Note: For data on U.S. citizens, see Table 8.7.

TABLE 10.72 Action Taken to Solve Local Problems, by National Origin, Excluding U.S. Citizens

Type of Action Taken	Mexican	Cuban
None	428	260
	80.6%	83.6%
Contacted government	20	9
	3.8%	2.9%
Acted with others	64	29
	12.1%	9.3%
Acted autonomously	19	13
	3.6%	4.2%
Total	531	311
	100.0%	100.0%

Note: For data on U.S. citizens, see Table 8.10.

TABLE 10.73   Involvement with Schools, by National Origin, Excluding U.S. Citizens

Activity	Mexican	Cuban
Met with teacher	231	155
	55.1%	55.8%
	(n=419)	(n=278)
Attended a PTA meeting	218	134
	40.9%	42.9%
	(n=533)	(n=312)
Met with school principal	248	141
	46.5%	45.2%
	(n=533)	(n=312)
Attended a school board meeting	104	59
	19.5%	18.9%
	(n=533)	(n=312)
Voted in a school board elections	152	72
	28.6%	23.1%
	(n=532)	(n=312)

Note: For data on U.S. citizens, see Table 8.12.

H. Ethnic Mutual Support (Tables 10.74–10.78)

Findings

While the majority of each national-origin group believed that they should help co-ethnics, a sizable minority—28 percent of Cubans and 23 percent of Mexicans—opposed this proposition (Table 10.74). Almost without exception, these Latino immigrants believed that they were helped by other Mexicans and Cubans (Table 10.75).

Two-thirds of both Mexicans and Cubans believed that general improvement among their co-ethnics helped them as individuals (Table 10.76).

Cuban and Mexican noncitizens differed in their belief in the value of elected officials of the respondent's national origin (Table 10.77). The majority of Mexicans agreed that Mexican-origin elected officials helped more than others. Cubans, on the other hand, were more evenly divided. Forty-six percent disagreed with the proposition and 41 percent agree that it was valuable to have Cuban elected officials.

Majorities of both the Mexican and the Cuban populations believed that government spending on programs to assist co-ethnics should increase (Table 10.78).

Questions Asked

125j, 133a, 133b, 133c, and 154.

TABLE 10.74 Should Co-Ethnics Help Each Other, by National Origin, Excluding U.S. Citizens

Co-Ethnics Should Help Other	Mexican	Cuban
Strongly agree	92	55
	22.0%	19.8%
Agree	207	131
	49.5%	47.1%
Neither agree nor disagree	25	15
	6.0%	5.4%
Disagree	82	68
	19.6%	24.5%
Strongly disagree	12	9
	2.9%	3.2%
Total	418	278
	100.0%	100.0%

Note: For data on U.S. citizens, see Table 9.1.

TABLE 10.75 Do Co-Ethnics Help or Hurt Each Other, by National Origin, Excluding U.S. Citizens

Perception	Mexican	Cuban
Help each other	249	152
	99.6%	98.1%
Pull each other down	1	3
	0.4%	1.9%
Total	250	155
	100.0%	100.0%

Note: For data on U.S. citizens, see Table 9.2.

TABLE 10.76   Do RGs Benefit if Co-Ethnics Do Well, by National Origin,
Excluding U.S. Citizens

Improvement for Co-Ethnics in General Helps Respondent	Mexican	Cuban
Strongly agree	73	41
	17.5%	14.7%
Agree	208	138
	49.8%	49.6%
Neither agree nor disagree	23	19
	5.5%	6.8%
Disagree	104	74
	24.9%	26.6%
Strongly disagree	10	6
	2.4%	2.2%
Total	418	278
	100.0%	100.0%

Note: For data on U.S. citizens, see Table 9.3.

TABLE 10.77   Level of Support from Co-Ethnic Officials, by National Origin,
Excluding U.S. Citizens

Co-Ethnic Officials Help More Than Non-Co-Ethnic Officials	Mexican	Cuban
Strongly agree	42	21
	10.1%	7.6%
Agree	177	93
	42.4%	33.5%
Neither agree nor disagree	41	35
	9.8%	12.6%
Disagree	145	121
	34.8%	43.5%
Strongly disagree	12	8
	2.9%	2.9%
Total	417	278
	100.0%	100.0%

Note: For data on U.S. citizens, see Table 9.4.

TABLE 10.78   Feelings about Government Spending on RG Programs, by National Origin, Excluding U.S. Citizens

Government Spending Should	Mexican	Cuban
Increase	308	192
	57.9%	61.3%
Be left the same	188	107
	35.3%	34.2%
Decrease	36	14
	6.8%	4.5%
Total	532	313
	100.0%	100.0%

Note: For data on U.S. citizens, see Table 9.18.

I. Ethnic Knowledge (Tables 10.79–10.82)

Findings

At least two-thirds of respondents were interested some or most of the time in activities involving co-ethnics (Table 10.79).

Few respondents could identify Mexican, Cuban, or Puerto Rican leaders (Table 10.80). Almost one-quarter of Cubans and Mexicans could identify Cesar Chavez. Seventeen percent of Cubans and 11 percent of Mexicans could identify the public office held by Xavier Suarez.

Ethnic-specific problems led the list of the most-important problem faced by the Mexican and Cuban communities (Table 10.81). The second- and third-most important issues were education and social issues.

The respondents felt that the solution to these issues lay with the government (Table 10.82).

Questions Asked

115, 116, 126, 131c, 131d, and 131e.

TABLE 10.79   Interest in RG Activities, by National Origin, Excluding U.S.
                   Citizens

Follow RG Activities	Mexican	Cuban
Most of the time	155	94
	37.9%	35.5%
Some of the time	127	82
	31.1%	30.9%
Now and then	82	62
	20.0%	23.4%
Hardly interested	45	27
	11.0%	10.2%
Total	409	265
	100.0%	100.0%

Note: For data on U.S. citizens, see Table 9.14.

TABLE 10.80   Recognition of Latino Leaders by National Origin, Excluding U.S.
                   Citizens

Leader (Correct or Partially Correct)	Mexican	Cuban
Cesar Chavez	128	78
	24.0%	24.9%
	(n=533)	(n=313)
Robert Garcia	23	18
	4.3%	5.7%
	(n=533)	(n=313)
Xavier Suarez	56	53
	10.6%	16.9%
	(n=533)	(n=313)

Note: For data on U.S. citizens, see Table 9.15.

TABLE 10.81 Main RG Problem, by National Origin, Excluding U.S. Citizens

Main RG Problem	Mexican	Cuban
Economics	47	27
	14.0%	13.0%
Social problems	62	37
	18.5%	17.8%
Health care issues	1	1
	0.3%	0.5%
Education	66	33
	19.6%	15.9%
Immigration	9	3
	2.7%	1.4%
Political issues	16	15
	4.8%	7.2%
Environmental issues	2	1
	0.6%	0.5%
Ethnic issues	124	85
	36.9%	40.9%
Moral issues	3	2
	0.9%	1.0%
Others	6	4
	1.8%	1.9%
Total	336	208
	100.0%	100.0%

Note: For data on U.S. citizens, see Table 9.16.

TABLE 10.82 Role of Government versus Individual in Solving Main RG Problem, by National Origin, Excluding U.S. Citizens

Who Should Solve RG Problem	Mexican	Cuban
Individual	83	59
	24.1%	27.2%
Government	262	158
	75.9%	72.8%
Total	345	217
	100.0%	100.0%

Note: For data on U.S. citizens, see Table 9.17.

J. Ethnic Bonds Among Latinos (Tables 10.83–10.86)

Findings

When asked about cultural similarities among Latinos, the majority took the middle ground (Table 10.83). Cuban and Mexican noncitizens were more likely to say that Latinos were not very similar than they are to say that they were very similar.

In pairings between Latino national-origin groups, Mexicans and Puerto Ricans, Mexicans and Cubans, and Puerto Ricans and Cubans, the most common response was that no two groups had very similar political concerns (Table 10.84-10.86). The majority of Cubans and Mexicans saw few similarities between the groups. The majority of Cubans also saw few similarities in political concerns between Puerto Ricans and Cubans.

Questions Asked

173, 174, 175, and 176.

TABLE 10.83 Belief in Common Latino Culture, by National Origin, Excluding U.S. Citizens

Degree of Similarity	Mexican	Cuban
Very similar	81	40
	19.4%	14.5%
Somewhat similar	232	167
	55.6%	60.5%
Not very similar	104	69
	24.9%	25.0%
Total	417	276
	100.0%	100.0%

Note: For data on U.S. citizens, see Table 9.19.

TABLE 10.84 Belief in Common Political Concerns of Mexicans and Puerto Ricans, by National Origin, Excluding U.S. Citizens

Degree of Similarity	Mexican	Cuban
Very similar	43	27
	10.7%	10.2%
Somewhat similar	165	110
	41.1%	41.4%
Not very similar	193	129
	48.1%	48.5%
Total	401	266
	100.0%	100.0%

Note: For data on U.S. citizens, see Table 9.20.

TABLE 10.85 Belief in Common Political Concerns of Mexicans and Cubans, by National Origin, Excluding U.S. Citizens

Degree of Similarity	Mexican	Cuban
Very similar	30	19
	7.5%	7.1%
Somewhat similar	163	101
	40.6%	37.8%
Not very similar	208	147
	51.9%	55.1%
Total	401	267
	100.0%	100.0%

Note: For data on U.S. citizens, see Table 9.21.

TABLE 10.86 Belief in Common Political Concerns of Cubans and Puerto Ricans, by National Origin, Excluding U.S. Citizens

Degree of Similarity	Mexican	Cuban
Very similar	48	27
	12.0%	10.1%
Somewhat similar	171	103
	42.6%	38.4%
Not very similar	182	138
	45.4%	51.5%
Total	401	268
	100.0%	100.0%

Note: For data on U.S. citizens, see Table 9.22

Appendix 1:
Abbreviated Version of the
Latino National Political
Survey Questionnaire

This appendix contains an abbreviated version of the Latino National Political Survey. The version presented here lists all questions asked of the respondents. It excludes all interviewer instructions and answers to some of the questions. Answers are not provided to questions that can be answered with a yes or a no, to open-ended questions, and to those where the answers are stated in the question.

The questions also asked of Anglos are marked with an asterisk.

1. Respondent's group
   Mexican   Puerto Rican   Cuban

*2. Sex of respondent
   Male   Female

*3. In what month, day, and year were you born?

4. Here is a list of names that are used to describe persons of Spanish heritage. Please tell me all of these, if any, you call yourself.

Mexican	Puerto Rican	Spanish
Mexicano(a)	Niuyorican/	Spanish American
Mexican American	Neorican	Raza
Chicano(a)	Hispanic	American
Cuban	Latino(a)	Hispano
		Other

5. Which one do you most prefer?

6. Different people use the term "Hispanic" to mean different things. What do you mean when you call yourself Hispanic?

7. Different people use the term "Latino" to mean different things. What do you mean when you call yourself Latino?

*8. Do you consider yourself
    White   Black   Other (specify)

*9. Are you currently
    Married   Widowed
    Living with someone   Never married
    Separated   Married, but not living with
    Divorced   spouse
    Single   Other (specify)

10. Is (your spouse/the person you live with) of
    Mexican origin   Other Latino origin
    Cuban origin   Anglo origin
    Puerto Rican origin   Some other origin

*11. Are you a parent or legal guardian of any children?

*12. Everyone may not have had the chance to go to school. In your case, what is the highest grade or year of school that you completed?

13. Did you get a high school diploma or pass a high school equivalency test?

*14. What is the highest degree that you have earned?

15. (Between grades one through twelve,) did you attend
    Public schools   Other private school
    Parochial schools   Any combination of these

16. During what grades did you attend parochial or private school?

17. If your parents had the opportunity to attend school, what is the highest grade or year of school that your father completed?

18. And your mother, what is the highest grade or year of school that she completed?

19. What was the highest grade or year of school completed by (your husband/your wife/the person you live with)?

*20a. What is your religious preference? That is, are you
    Catholic   No preference
    Protestant   Something else
    Jewish

20b. What denomination is that?

Protestant	Jehovah's Witness
Baptist	Christian
Methodist	Evangelical
Lutheran	Church of Christ
Presbyterian	Anglican
Episcopalian	Mormon
Pentecostal	Something else

*21. Some people have had deep religious experiences that have transformed their lives. I'm thinking of experiences sometimes described as "being born again in one's faith" or "discovering Jesus Christ in one's life." There are deeply religious people who have not had an experience of this sort. How about you, have you had such an experience?

*22. Would you say your religion provides

A great deal of guidance	Some guidance
Quite a bit of guidance	No daily guidance

*23. How often do you attend religious services? Do you attend

Almost every week or more	A few times a year
Once or twice a month	Almost never
	Never

*24. Please tell me which of these statements best describes your present work situation:

Working full-time (35 hours or more per week)
Working part-time (less than 35 hours per week)
Have a job but not at work because of temporary illness, laid off, or on leave
Work occasionally, temporary jobs
Unemployed and looking for work
Unemployed and not looking for work
In school
Retired
Homemaker or something else

25a. Who do you work for? (In what city and state is that located?)

*25b. In what kind of business or industry (do/did) you work?

*26a. What is your occupation? (What sort of work do you do?)

*26b. What are your main duties?

*27. Do your duties involve supervising others?

28. Please tell me which of these statements best describes the present work situation of (your husband/your wife/the person you are living with):
    Working full-time (35 hours or more per week)
    Working part-time (less than 35 hours per week)
    Have a job but not at work because of temporary illness, laid
        off, or on leave
    Work occasionally, temporary jobs
    Unemployed and looking for work
    Unemployed and not looking for work
    In school
    Retired
    Homemaker or something else

*29. Do you
    Rent your home
    Own your home
    Live here under some other type of living arrangement

30. Do your parents rent or own their home?
    Rent   Own
    Other

*31. Did you serve on active duty in the U.S. Armed Forces?

*32. During what years did you serve?

33. Now I'd like to ask you about your family origins. In what country was your father born?

34. In what country was his father born?

35. And you father's mother, in what country was she born?

36. Now about your mother—in what country was your mother born?

37. What about her mother, in what country was she born?

38. And your mother's father, in what country was he born?

*39. In what country were you born?
    The United States   Mexico
    Cuba   Puerto Rico
                                 Other

40. How old were you when you came to this country to stay?

41. If you had an opportunity to go to school, what grades or years of school had you completed at the time that you came to the United States?

42. Which of these, if any, are reasons that you came to the U.S.?
    To join family members   For economic reasons
    To flee political problems   Because your family brought you
    For any other reason

*43. Now we would like to ask about U.S. citizenship. Are you
    A U.S. citizen
    Currently applying for citizenship
    Planning to apply for citizenship
    Not planning to become a citizen

44. What is the main reason for this?

45. Do you plan
    To remain permanently in the U.S.
    To return to your country

*46. How strong is your love for the United States?
    Extremely strong   Very strong
    Somewhat strong   Not very strong

*47. How proud are you to be an American?
    Extremely proud   Very proud
    Somewhat proud   Not very proud

*48. In general, which, if any, do you rely on most for news about politics and public affairs:
    Television   Magazines
    Newspapers   Radio

49. Is that in English, in Spanish, or both?
    English   Spanish
    Both

*50. Besides (Q. 48), which do you rely on the most for news about politics and public affairs?
    Television   Magazines
    Newspapers   Radio

51. Is that in English, in Spanish, or both?
    English   Spanish
    Both

*52. How many times during the past week did you watch national network news on TV?

*53. How many days during the past week did you read about politics and public affairs in a daily newspaper?

*54. Would you say you follow what's going on in politics and public affairs?

Most of the time	Some of the time
Only now and then	Hardly at all
	Never

55–59. Please tell me the names of any organizations or associations that you belong to or have given money or goods to in the past twelve months that are

*55. Unions, associations, or groups associated with work, businesses, or professions?
Names of organizations
Have you given money or goods in the past twelve months?
Are you a member?
Are you an active member? That is, do you regularly attend
    meetings and participate in the activities of the organization?

*56. Charities, religious organizations, or other organizations that look after people such as the elderly, handicapped children, or similar groups?
Names of organizations
Have you given money or goods in the past twelve months?
Are you a member?
Are you an active member?

*57. Social issue organizations, such as reducing taxes, protecting the environment, promoting prayer in schools, or any other cause.
Names of organizations
Have you given money or goods in the past twelve months?
Are you a member?
Are you an active member?

*58. Sports, recreation, community, neighborhood, school, cultural, or youth organizations.
Names of organizations
Have you given money or goods in the past twelve months?
Are you a member?
Are you an active member?

59. Hispanic organizations.
    Names of organizations
    Have you given money or goods in the past twelve months?
    Are you a member?
    Are you an active member?

60. In general, are the members of the organization(s) you belong to
    Mostly [RG]
    [RG] and Anglos (White Americans)
    Mostly Anglos
    Something else

61. Is there any group or organization that you think looks out for your concerns, even if you are not a member?

62. What group or organization is that?

63. Thinking about [RG]s, even if you are not a member, is there any group or organization that you think looks out for [RG] concerns?

64. What group or organization is that?

*65. Now I would like to ask you some questions about contacts you may have had with local, state, or national government offices. In the past twelve months, have you contacted by letter, telephone, or in person a government office about a problem or to get help or information?

*66. What was the reason for this contact?

*67. The last time you contacted a government office, did you
    Contact the office on your own
    Ask someone to help you or go with you

68. What kind of help did you want this person to give you?

69. Was the official you contacted
    An [RG]   An Anglo (White American)
    Something else

*70. How satisfied were you with the results of your contacts?
    Very satisfied   Satisfied
    Not satisfied

*71. Do you feel that
    You were treated as well as anyone would have been
    Other people were treated better than you

*72. We would like to ask you about elections in the United States. During 1988, did anyone talk to you about registering to vote?

*73. Who spoke to you about registering to vote in the U.S.?

*74. Have you ever been registered to vote in the U.S.?

*75. Are you currently registered to vote in the U.S.?

76. Are you registered at your current address in the U.S.?

77. Please give me the name and address that appear on your voter registration form.

*78. When we talk to people about elections, we find that a lot of people were not able to vote because they weren't old enough, they weren't registered, they weren't interested, they were sick, or they just didn't have the time. How about you, did you vote in the elections in November 1988?

79. When you went to vote in the presidential elections in November 1988, as far as you know, was there a Spanish-language ballot?

80. Did you use the Spanish ballot, the English ballot, or both?
    Only English   Only Spanish
    Both

81. Has the availability of Spanish ballots made it easier for you to vote?

82. Did an election official or a representative of a political party explain voting procedures or how to use the ballot in Spanish when you went to vote in 1988 or when you voted most recently?

*83. For whom did you vote for president in 1988?
    George Bush   Another candidate
    Michael Dukakis   Voted, but not for president

*84. Did you vote for a candidate for the U.S. House of Representatives in 1988?

*85. Was the candidate you voted for
    A Republican   A Democrat   Something else

*86. Did you vote in the U.S. House of Representatives election of 1986?

87. Did you vote in the presidential election of 1984?

88. When an [RG] runs for office, are you
    More likely to vote   Less likely to vote
    It make no difference

*89. Have you ever had the opportunity to vote for an [RG] in an election in the United States?

*90. Think about the most recent election you voted in when an [RG]/Hispanic ran against an Anglo. Did you vote
    For the [RG]/Hispanic   For the Anglo
    For another candidate

*91. At the time of the November 1988 elections, do you remember which candidate you preferred for president? Was it
    George Bush   Another candidate
    Michael Dukakis   None of the candidates

*92. Do you consider yourself
    A Democrat   An independent
    A Republican   Something else

*93. Would you call yourself
    A strong Democrat
    A not very strong Democrat

*94. Have you
    Always considered yourself a Democrat
    Identified with the Republican party in the past

*95. Would you call yourself
    A strong Republican
    A not very strong Republican

*96. Have you
    Always considered yourself a Republican
    Identified with the Democratic party in the past

*97. Do you now think of yourself as
    Closer to the Republican party
    Closer to the Democratic party

98. Regarding the 1988 election in the U.S., do you remember which candidate for president you preferred at the time? Was it
    George Bush   Another candidate
    Michael Dukakis   None of the candidates

99. Regarding U.S. political parties, do you consider yourself
    A Democrat   An independent
    A Republican   Something else

*100. Do you think there are important differences in what the Republicans and the Democrats stand for?

*101. What do you think the Republicans stand for?

*102. What do you think the Democrats stand for?

*103. Now I would like to ask some different kinds of questions. Over the past month, have you had to do any of the following as part of your job:
    Write a letter
    Make a telephone call to someone you do not know personally
    Take part in a meeting where decisions are made
    Give a presentation or talk
    Get in touch with government officials

*104. Do you happen to be personally acquainted with an elected or appointed official who could help you with a personal or community problem?

105. If you wanted to go to a meeting—for example, a school or community meeting, or a meeting at your church—how difficult would it be to arrange for someone to help you with your responsibilities at home? Would it be
    Very difficult   Somewhat difficult
    Not difficult

*106. Here are some ways that people get involved in the schools. Other than when you were a student, have you
    Met with a teacher or teachers
    Attended a PTA meeting
    Met with a school principal
    Attended a meeting of the school board
    Voted in a school board election

*107. Next, I have some questions about trust and satisfaction with government. How much of the time do you think you can trust government officials to do what is right?
    Just about always   Some of the time
    Most of the time   Almost never

*108. Would you say that the government generally is
    Run by a few people looking out for their own interests
    Run for the benefit of all

*109. What do you say is the most important problem facing people in this country today?

*110. Which of the following two statements best describes your views about this problem?
    A lot of progress can be made on this problem without involving the government.
    In order to make substantial progress on this problem, the government will have to get involved.

*111. What do you think is the most important problem facing people in your (city/county)?

*112. Which of the following two statements best describes your views about this problem?
    A lot of progress can be made on this problem without involving the government.
    In order to make substantial progress on this problem, the government will have to get involved.

*113. During the last two weeks, have you talked to anyone about these local or national problems?

*114. Whom did you talk to?

115. Last, what do you think is the one most-important problem facing [RG]s?

116. Which of the following statements best describes your views about this problem?
    A lot of progress can be made on this problem without involving the government.
    In order to make substantial progress on this problem, the government will have to get involved.

117. During the past two weeks, have you talked to anyone about this problem?

118. Whom did you talk to about this problem?

*119. Now I'd like to ask you about some things you may have done in the last year. During the past twelve months, have you worked or cooperated with others to try to solve a problem affecting your city or neighborhood?

120. Was this a problem particularly affecting [RG]s?

*121. What problem was that?

*122. What did you do?

*123. How satisfied were you with the results of your effort?
     Very satisfied   Unsatisfied
     Satisfied   Very unsatisfied

*124. We would like to find out about some of the things people in the U.S. do
     to make their views known. Which of the activities listed on this card, if
     any, have you done in the past twelve months?
          Signed a petition regarding an issue or problem that concerns you
          Written a letter, telephoned, or sent a telegram to an editor or public
             official regarding issues that concern you
          Attended a public meeting
          Worn a campaign button, put a campaign sticker on your car, or
             placed a sign in your window or in front of your house
          Gone to any political meetings, rallies, speeches, or dinners in
             support of a particular candidate
          Worked either for pay or on a volunteer basis for a party or a
             candidate running for office
          Contributed money to an individual candidate, a political party, or
             some other political organization supporting a candidate or an
             issue in an election

*125. Now we would like to ask you about your views on various types of
     government programs. As I read each program, tell me if you would
     like to see it increased even if it meant paying more taxes, if you would
     like to see it decreased, or if you would leave it the same.
          Improving and protecting the environment
          Public education
          Public assistance or welfare
          Medical or health care
          Programs to support science and technology
          Child care services
          Programs to help legal immigrants and refugees
          Defense spending
          Crime control and drug prevention
          Programs to help [RG]s
          Programs to help blacks

126. Some people follow what is going on with [RG]s most of the time.
     Others aren't that interested. Would you say that you follow what is
     going on with [RG]s
               Most of the time   Only now and then
               Some of the time   Hardly at all
                                             Never

127. I am going to read a list of things that [RG]s may do together to increase their influence or to get something done within the United States. As I read each activity, tell me if you have done this activity during the past twelve months.

    Worked as a volunteer or for pay for a candidate endorsed by [RGs] or leaders

    Worked with [RG]s to get [RG]s to vote as a group

    Signed a petition in support of [RG] concerns

    Boycotted a company or a product in support of [RG] concerns

    Attended a public meeting/demonstration regarding [RG] concerns

    Worked on projects that help maintain or promote [RG] culture, history, or art

    Written a letter, telephoned, or sent a telegram to an editor or public official regarding issues concerning [RG]s

    Contributed money to an [RG] candidate, to an [RG] organization, or to support other [RG] activities

*128. We would like your opinion on some issues that have been talked about in recent months. On each card, the number 1 represents a position held by some people, the number 5 represents an opposing position, and the numbers 2 through 4 stand for positions between these two. Please indicate the number that best represents your opinion on each issue.

    1. The government should provide jobs for everyone who wants a job.
    5. It's up to each person to get his or her own job.

*129.
    1. Individuals should provide their own housing.
    5. The government should provide housing to anyone who needs it.

*130.
    1. The government should guarantee every person or family a minimum income, even if no one in the family can work.
    5. People should work and earn their own income.

*131. Now we have some questions concerning various public figures.

    What job or political office does Dan Quayle hold now?

    How about William Rehnquist? What job or political office does he hold now?

    What position or job does Cesar Chavez hold now?

    What position or job does Robert "Bobby" Garcia hold now?

    What position or job does Xavier Suarez hold now?

*132. Which party has the most members in the U.S. House of Representatives?

133. Next we would like to know how strongly you agree or disagree with the following statements:

133a. [RG]s have an obligation to work with other [RG]s to increase the
       number of [RG] elected and appointed officials.
       Strongly agree   Disagree
       Agree   Strongly disagree

133b. As things get better for [RG]s in general, things also get better for me.
       Strongly agree   Disagree
       Agree   Strongly disagree

*134. Another issue we would like to ask you about is international affairs
       and foreign relations. Some people say that the U.S. government should
       begin immediately to reestablish diplomatic relations with Cuba. Others
       are opposed to this. What do you think?
       Begin immediately to reestablish relations
       The U.S. should not establish relations

*135. Some people want Puerto Rico to become a state, others want it to
       become independent, and still others want it to remain as it is, a
       Commonwealth. What do you think?
       Become a state   Become independent
       Remain as Commonwealth

*136. Some people say that U.S. policies are a major cause of Mexico's
       economic crisis; others say that governmental corruption and ineffi-
       ciency in Mexico are an even greater cause of Mexico's problems. Which
       do you think is a greater problem for Mexico?
       U.S. policies
       Governmental corruption and inefficiency in Mexico

 137. Some [RG]s are more concerned about government and politics in [RG's
       country] than in the U.S. Others are more concerned about government
       and politics in the U.S. How about you? Are you
       More concerned about government and politics in [RG country]
       More concerned about government and politics in the U.S.
       Equally concerned about both

*138. I am going to read the names of some countries. Rate each country
       using this feeling thermometer. You may use any number from 1 to 100
       for rating. Ratings between 50 degrees and 100 degrees mean that you
       feel favorable and warm toward the country. Ratings between 0 and 50
       degrees mean that you don't feel too favorable toward the country. If
       we come to a country you don't recognize, you don't need to rate that
       one. Just tell me and we'll move on to the next one. If you do recognize

a country but don't feel particularly warm or cold towards it, you would rate the country at 50 degrees.

Russia or the Soviet Union	England/Great Britain
Mexico	Cuba
Puerto Rico	Venezuela
Japan	Israel
Nicaragua	United States

*139. We are interested in how people are getting along financially these days. Would you say you (and your family living with you) are
   Much better off financially than twelve months ago
   Better off financially than twelve months ago
   The same financially than twelve months ago
   Worse off financially than twelve months ago
   Much worse off financially than twelve months ago

*140. Now looking ahead, do you think that twelve months from now you (and your family living with you) will be
   Much better off financially
   Better off financially
   The same financially
   Worse off financially
   Much worse off financially

141. Tell us how strongly you agree or disagree with the following statements.

141a. Our society should do whatever is necessary to make sure that everyone has an equal opportunity to succeed.
   Strongly agree   Disagree
   Agree   Strongly disagree

141b. It is OK if some people have more of a chance in life than others.
   Strongly agree   Disagree
   Agree   Strongly disagree

*142. We hear a lot of talk these days about liberals and conservatives. Here is a seven-point scale on which the political views that people might hold are arranged from very liberal to very conservative. Where would you place yourself on this scale?
   Very liberal   Slightly conservative
   Liberal   Conservative
   Slightly liberal   Very conservative
   Moderate, middle of the road

*143. What about Jesse Jackson? What would you call him?
        Very liberal   Slightly conservative
        Liberal   Conservative
        Slightly liberal   Very conservative
        Moderate, middle of the road

*144. And what would you call Ronald Reagan?
        Very liberal   Slightly conservative
        Liberal   Conservative
        Slightly liberal   Very conservative
        Moderate, middle of the road

*145. There are many controversial groups in the United States. From the groups that I name and the ones that you think of, name the one group that you dislike the most. Is it
        the Communist party   Black Muslims
        the Nazi party   English Only, U.S. English
        the Ku Klux Klan   Atheist organizations
        Gay and Lesbian groups   Some other group

*146. Tell us how strongly you agree or disagree with the following statements.

146a. Members of (group from 145) should not be allowed to hold elective office in the US.
        Strongly agree   Disagree
        Agree   Strongly disagree

146b. Members of (group from 145) should be allowed to teach in public schools.
        Strongly agree   Disagree
        Agree   Strongly disagree

146c. (Group from 145) should be allowed to hold public rallies in our city.
        Strongly agree   Disagree
        Agree   Strongly disagree

147. Some people think that the U.S. government should be more involved in the internal affairs of Central American countries. Others think it should be less involved in this area. What do you think? Do you think that the U.S. should be
        More involved   Less involved

148. Which do you think is the greater cause of unrest in Central America today:
        Subversion (stirring up trouble) from Cuba, Nicaragua, and the Soviet Union
        Poverty and lack of human rights in the area

149. Because you are an [RG], have you ever been turned down as a renter or buyer of a home, or been treated rudely in a restaurant, or been denied a job, or experienced other important types of discrimination?

*150. Now I would like to ask you about how much discrimination or unfair treatment you think different groups face in the U.S. Do you think the following groups face a lot of discrimination, some, a little, or no discrimination at all?

  Blacks   Mexican-origin people
  Puerto Ricans   Cuban Americans
  Women   Jewish Americans
  Asian Americans (such as Chinese, Japanese, and Koreans)

151. There has been some discussion about abortion during recent years. Which one of the statements on the card best agrees with your view? By law

  Abortion should never be permitted
  Abortion should be permitted only in case of rape, incest, or when the woman's life is in danger
  An abortion should be permitted but only after the need for abortion has been clearly established
  A woman should always be able to obtain an abortion as a matter of personal choice

*152. Generally speaking, would you say that
  Most people can be trusted
  You must be very careful in dealing with people

*153. Would you say that most of the time
  People try to be helpful
  They are mostly looking out for themselves

154. Some [RG]s say that [RG]s usually try to help each other get ahead. Other [RG]s say that, instead of helping each other, [RG]s usually pull each other down so that no one gets ahead. What do you think? Do [RG]s

  Help each other   Pull each other down

155. For persons convicted of murder, do you favor or oppose the death penalty?

  Favor   Oppose
  Depends

156. Tell me how strongly you agree with the following statements.
156a. Success in life is pretty much determined by forces outside our control.

  Strongly agree   Disagree
  Agree   Strongly disagree

156b. Hard work does not necessarily lead to success.
   Strongly agree   Disagree
   Agree   Strongly disagree

157–160. The following statements cover issues that are in the news these days. In each scale, the number 1 represents a position held by some people, the number 5 represents an opposing position, and the numbers 2 through 4 stand for positions between these two. Please indicate the number that best represents your opinion on each issue.

*157. 1. In general, women will be better off if they stay home and raise families
   5. In general, women will be better off if they have careers and jobs just like men.

158. 1. Men in public office are more capable than women of making decisions in time of crisis
   5. Women in public office are more capable than men of making decisions in time of crisis

159. 1. Even if it limits their opportunity for advancement in job or career, women should help their husbands by taking care of household chores and children.
   5. Even if it limits their opportunity for advancement in job or career, men should help their wives by taking care of household chores and children.

*160. 1. The government should establish quotas in college admissions and job hiring to ensure [RC]/Hispanic representation†
   5. College admission and job hiring should be based strictly on merit.
   †When asked of Anglos, this question stated: "to ensure Hispanic representation."

*161. Now we would like to ask you about some other issues that some people have been discussing lately.

161a. Laws should be passed making English the official language of this country.
   Strongly agree   Disagree
   Agree   Strongly disagree

161b. Government agencies should provide services in Spanish and other languages to non-English-speaking clients.
   Strongly agree   Disagree
   Agree   Strongly disagree

161c. Businesses have the right to require that employees speak English during working hours.
    Strongly agree   Disagree
    Agree   Strongly disagree

161d. All citizens and residents of the U.S. should learn English.
    Strongly agree   Disagree
    Agree   Strongly disagree

162. Should [RG] children in U.S. schools study the history and culture of
    Only the United States
    Both the United States and (RG's country), but more about the United States
    Both the United States and (RG's country) equally
    Both the United States and (RG's country), but more about (RG's country)
    Only study the history and culture of (RG's country)

163. How strongly do you support or oppose bilingual education?
    Strongly support it   Oppose it
    Support it   Strongly oppose it
    Feel uncertain about it

164. Would you be willing to pay more taxes to expand bilingual education?

165. What do you mean by "bilingual education"?

166. Have you or a member of your family participated in a bilingual education program?

*167. We would also like to ask you some questions about your views on immigration. Tell us how strongly you agree or disagree with the following statements.

167a. Latin Americans should have preference over people from other countries who want to emigrate to the U.S.
    Strongly agree   Disagree
    Agree   Strongly disagree

167b. There are too many immigrants coming to this country.
    Strongly agree   Disagree
    Agree   Strongly disagree

167c. If a citizen and an immigrant apply for the same job, the citizen should be hired.
    Strongly agree   Disagree
    Agree   Strongly disagree

168. What language do you usually speak at home?
     Only Spanish   More English than Spanish
     More Spanish than   Only English
       English   Both languages equally

169. Considering your abilities in understanding, speaking, reading, and
     writing English or Spanish, which of these statements best describes
     your abilities in Spanish? Would you say that you
     Don't know Spanish   Are no different in either
       language   Are better in Spanish
     Are much better in English   Are much better in Spanish
     Are better in English   Don't know English language

170. When you go to social gatherings or parties, are the people there usually
     All [RG]s   More Anglos than [RG]s
     More [RG]s than Anglos   All Anglos
     About half and half

171. At the present time, are your friends
     All [RG]s   More Anglos than [RG]s
     More [RG]s than Anglos   All Anglos
     About half and half

172. Are the people at the places where you go to relax or just to have fun
     All [RG]s   More Anglos than [RG]s
     More [RG]s than Anglos   All Anglos
     About half and half

173. Some [RG]s say all Hispanics or Latinos in the U.S. have a great deal in
     common culturally. Others say that there are many cultural differences
     among Hispanics. Do you think that [RG]s and other Hispanics are
     culturally
     Very similar   Somewhat similar
     Not very similar

174. Some people say that Mexican-origin people, Puerto Ricans, and
     Cubans in the U.S. have many concerns in common. Do you think that
     the political concerns of Mexican-origin people and Puerto Ricans are
     Very similar   Somewhat similar
     Not very similar

175. How about Mexican-origin people and Cubans in the U.S.? Do you
     think that the political concerns of these two groups are
     Very similar   Somewhat similar
     Not very similar

176. What about Puerto Ricans and Cubans in the U.S.? Do you think that the political concerns of these two groups are
    Very similar   Somewhat similar
    Not very similar

177. If respondent is of Mexican origin ask: (Other than your family,) how much contact do you have with people of Mexican origin? Is it
    A lot of contact   A little contact
    Some contact   No contact

178. If respondent is of Puerto Rican origin ask: (Other than your family,) how much contact do you have with Puerto Ricans? Is it
    A lot of contact   A little contact
    Some contact   No contact

179. If respondent is of Cuban origin ask: (Other than your family,) how much contact do you have with Cubans? Is it
    A lot of contact   A little contact
    Some contact   No contact

*180. Next, we have a few more questions about your household. By members of your household, we mean those people who live with you and who share common expenses. This could include parents, grandparents, spouses, children, brothers and sisters, and other relatives and persons. How many people lived in your household in 1988?

*181. And how many of these worked for pay in 1988?

*182. Please tell me the total yearly income received by you and other members of your household in 1988. Include money received by all members of your household from all sources such as work, social security payments, child support, welfare payments, rent, interest, and anything else. What is the total yearly income received by you and the other members of your household in 1988 before taxes?

SAQ1. Please rate each group using the feeling thermometer. Ratings between 50 degrees and 100 degrees mean that you feel favorable toward the group. The ratings between 0 degrees and 50 degrees mean that you feel unfavorable toward the group.
    Mexican Americans   Puerto Ricans in Puerto Rico
    Mexican immigrants   Anglos (white Americans)
    Blacks   Cubans in the U.S.
    Puerto Ricans in the U.S.   Jewish Americans
    Asians Americans (such as Chinese, Japanese, and Koreans)

SAQ2. We also want to know how easy or difficult it is to use Spanish [or
English, depending on questionnaire used]. Please translate the phrases
below. If you prefer, the interviewer can read them to you.

He raises his hand (El [levanta/alza] [las/sus] manos).

It is very cold (Hace mucho frio/Esta muy frio).

The door is not open (La puerta no esta abierta).

She is playing with her doll (Ella [juega/esta jugando] con su
[muneca/mona]).

There is a horse near the church (Hay un caballo cerca de la iglesia).

She writes with chalk (Ella escribe con tiza)

guilt/blame/fault (culpa; culpabilidad)

surplus/excess/excessive (exceso; excedente; sobra; sobrante/
demasia)

glance/look (mirada; ojeada; vistazo)

Appendix 2:
Latino National Political Survey Methodology

Robert Santos

Overview

The Latino National Political Survey measures the political attitudes and behaviors of three specific groups of Latinos in the United States: Mexicans, Puerto Ricans, and Cubans. The survey objectives called for a national area probability sample of households to yield data about political attitudes and behaviors from one-hour interviews completed with eight hundred Mexican, six hundred Puerto Rican, and six hundred Cuban adults, as well as seven hundred non-Latinos, with a geographic Latino population coverage rate of at least 85 percent. This meant, for instance, that the selection of Puerto Ricans would expand beyond the New York Metropolitan Area. The LNPS relied on face-to-face data collection using a Spanish or English version of the survey instrument.

We designed and executed the sample in the first six months of 1989. The geographic area of coverage for this survey included at least 90 percent of the Mexican, Cuban, and Puerto Rican populations. The sample used a multistage area probability sample design based on 1980 census data.

We sampled areas, or Primary Sampling Units (PSUs), at the first stage of selection. PSUs consisted of groups of contiguous metropolitan counties, Standard Metropolitan Statistical Areas (SMSAs), and groups of rural counties. Forty PSUs were used in the survey, of which twenty-eight were self-representing (i.e., areas with so large a Latino population that they would be included in all samples of forty areas).

We selected the remaining twelve non-self-representing areas with probabilities proportional to Latino population counts (pps). Selection probabilities employed weighted measures of size that reflected the oversampling of Cubans and Puerto Ricans relative to the Mexican population. Twelve areas were selected using a highly stratified paired-selections technique called controlled selection. Stratification factors included metropolitan status, geography (state/region), and concentration of the Latino population.

At the second stage of selection, we selected a total of 550 secondary sampling units (SSUs) consisting of Census Block Groups or Enumeration Districts with pps from the PSUs. Stratification for the SSU design included density of Latino population and geography. Higher-density Latino neighborhoods were oversampled by a factor of 3 to 1 relative to the lowest-density areas. The SSU design also featured a sampling stratum to detect the birth and expansion of Latino neighborhoods since 1980. The LNPS included twenty SSUs from this stratum.

Within each SSU, we selected a smaller tertiary unit, a Listing Area (LA) with pps. LAs were formed by taking contiguous blocks and grouping them into geographic units that maintained a prespecified minimum measure of size.

We sent enumerators to list the addresses of housing units (HUs) found in each LA. The sample of households selected for the LNPS was drawn from these lists in such a way as to produce the desired overall sampling fraction for that area.

We assigned addresses to interviewers in the sample and obtained a household listing of the residents as well as their ages and ethnicity. We defined Latinos (Mexican, Puerto Rican, Cuban) to be those individuals who reported at least one parent or at least two grandparents as being solely of Mexican, Cuban, or Puerto Rican ancestry. When more than one adult (eighteen or over) Latino resided in a household, one was randomly selected to be the survey respondent. A random subsample of addresses was targeted for the non-Latino portion of the sample, and here there was no ethnicity restriction.

The LNPS featured a two-phase sample design. This was necessary because the survey experienced a higher-than-expected Latino eligibility rate, especially for Mexicans. In October of 1989, after about two-thirds of the final interviews had been completed on the sample, we determined that the overall sampling rate should be adjusted downward to minimize the possibility of cost overruns, yet ensure that the Latino interview targets were attained or achieved. The second phase of the sample, therefore, consisted of the stratified random subsampling of half the SSUs. A random half sample was retained in the study, and all of its sample addresses were brought to a final disposition. We ceased fieldwork on the nonfinal addresses in the other half sample.

The principal period of data collection spanned July 1989 through March 1990 (although 19 interviews were collected afterward). We conducted 2,817 Latino interviews and 598 non-Latino interviews. Of the Latino total, 1,546 were Mexican, 589 were Puerto Rican, and 682 were Cuban. Thus, apart from the non-Latino portion of the sample, we achieved or exceeded the interview targets for the survey.

We attained a screening response rate of 90 percent. The Latino interview response rate reached 82 percent; the non-Latino interview response rate was 62 percent. Thus, Latinos achieved an overall response rate of 74 percent, whereas the overall response rate among non-Latinos was 56 percent. Again, apart from the non-Latino sample, we achieved the survey goals.

We conducted 60 percent of the Latino interviews in Spanish. Latino interviews conducted in English averaged 83 minutes, while those in Spanish averaged 91 minutes. Non-Latino interviews averaged one hour.

In order to analyze the survey data, we generated weights that reflect selection probabilities and incorporate adjustments for nonresponse and poststratification.

The Sample Design

Population Definition

The survey objectives specifically target Mexican, Puerto Rican, and Cuban Latino subgroups for inclusion in the study. Other Latinos, while in aggregate composing a significant percentage of the total Latino population (20 percent), comprise several smaller subgroups (e.g., Nicaraguans, Dominicans, Colombians, Guatemalans). We presumed these groups to be especially heterogeneous in relation to the study subject matter. Moreover, the costs of sampling sufficient numbers of these groups for separate analysis were quite high and subject to high variability because of their rareness in the population. Consequently, we included only Mexicans, Puerto Ricans, and Cubans in the "Latino" part of the survey.

For this study, a Latino (i.e., Mexican, Cuban, or Puerto Rican) is defined as one who meets the following criteria: (1) at least one parent must be solely of Mexican or Cuban or Puerto Rican ancestry; or (2) at least two (any two) grandparents must be solely of Mexican or Cuban or Puerto Rican ancestry.

The screening process elicited the names, ages, and ethnicity of household residents. We did not attempt any interviews without a complete household listing, the establishment of survey eligibility, and (when necessary) the random selection of a respondent from among those eligible in the household. "Non-Latinos" included everyone who was not Mexican, Cuban, or Puerto Rican.[1]

Latino Coverage

A principal design issue in the LNPS was Latino population coverage. Coverage refers to the portion of the population of inference that receives a nonzero chance of selection through the sample design. In the LNPS, the principal source of noncoverage resulted from explicit geographic area exclusions from the sampling frame.

Deleting specific geographic areas of the United States from the sampling frame is a prudent and natural first step of any rare element survey, provided that the resulting population coverage is sustained at a high level. We examined 1980 census data from SMSAs and rural counties to determine levels of noncoverage.

First, we tabulated the distribution of Latinos by state and Latino type; we then assembled SMSAs and rural counties into two state-level categories. The first category included low Latino-incidence areas: Alaska and Hawaii, New England states (except Massachusetts and Connecticut), West North Central states (except Kansas), South Atlantic states (except Florida), East South Central states, specific West South Central states (Arkansas and Louisiana); specific Mountain states (Montana, Idaho, and Wyoming), and Washington, D.C. The second category included higher Latino incidence states. The twenty-one states in this category include Middle Atlantic states; East North Central states; specific West

---

[1] The non-Latinos reported on in this volume are not the entire sample of non-Latinos; see Chapter 1.

South Central states (Texas and Oklahoma); Pacific states; specific Mountain states (Utah, Colorado, Arizona, and New Mexico); and other states (Connecticut, Massachusetts, Florida, and Kansas). Note that when an SMSA in category 2 contained a constituent county that fell into a state listed under category 1, the entire collection of counties for that SMSA was placed in category 2.

All rural counties in category 1 above were deleted from the LNPS sampling frame. We included category 1 SMSAs in the sampling frame if they met the following criteria: the 1980 population count of a single Latino group (i.e., Mexican, Cuban, Puerto Rican) was three thousand or more, and the population concentration of that group exceeded 1 percent of the total population. These criteria caused four SMSAs in category 1 to be included in the LNPS sampling frame: Des Moines, Iowa; Fayetteville, North Carolina; Las Vegas, Nevada; and Omaha, Nebraska.

We included SMSAs in the LNPS frame if they satisfied one of the following rules: the SMSA met the inclusion criteria employed in category 1 or the 1980 population count of a single Latino type for the SMSA exceeded ten thousand. We included rural counties in category 2 if the 1980 population concentration for a single Latino type exceeded 10 percent of the total population.

These inclusion criteria yield a geographic area that achieved over 90 percent coverage for each of the Mexican, Puerto Rican, and Cuban populations. Three hundred eighty-two counties made up the LNPS frame. Table A-1 presents the attained coverage rates, by Latino subgroup.

Two additional comments are relevant to Latino population coverage in the LNPS. First, data from Hispanic voter polls in the Southwest suggest that Latino political behavior is related to an area's Latino population density. Latinos in high-density Latino areas behave differently from those in lower-density Latino areas. Since a significant proportion of Latinos reside in neighborhoods with low (less than 15 percent) Latino population density, it was imperative that the LNPS coverage area include a high proportion (over 90 percent) of the Latino population at the first stage of selection. This ensured that Latinos in neighborhoods of all densities would be represented, and presumably tapped the diverse political attitudes and behaviors of Latinos.

A second comment relates to another source of noncoverage in the LNPS

TABLE A-1 Coverage of the LNPS Sampling Frame, by Latino Subpopulation

Latino Subpopulation	Covered by LNPS Sampling Frame (%)	Noncoverage Incurred (%)	Total
Mexican	91.0	9.0	100% (8,740,439)
Puerto Rican	90.2	9.8	100% (2,013,945)
Cuban	91.5	8.5	100% (800,226)

sampling frame: the second stage of selection. Regular Secondary Sampling Units were included in the "regular" SSU sampling frame if their Latino population density exceeded a minimum threshold (usually 3 percent, but sometimes 5 percent). Although Latinos residing outside these areas were represented using a "new growth" stratum, a small amount of noncoverage is expected to remain at the second stage.

Setting Sampling Fractions

Ideally, the sampling fractions for the three Latino subpopulations would be based on the distribution of the population across the Latino density strata used for disproportionate sampling. Time and computing resource constraints did not permit the collection of those data. Instead, we based initial sampling fractions on 1980 housing unit counts by Latino subgroup.

Using 1980 census counts of households by Latino type, we set overall sampling fractions for Mexicans, Puerto Ricans, and Cubans. The sampling rates assumed a 90 percent population coverage and an overall 70 percent response rate. Thus, the number of Mexican households to be sampled was $800/[(0.9) \times (0.7)] = 1,270$. Using the same assumptions, we had to select 952 Cuban and 952 Puerto Rican households. In thousands, the 1980 household counts for Mexicans, Puerto Ricans, and Cubans was 2,227, 599, and 279, respectively. Taking the ratio of desired to total households (with some rounding) yielded the following overall sampling rates by Latino type:

Mexican	1 in 1,800
Puerto Rican	1 in 630
Cuban	1 in 300

These sampling rates show that, on average, Cubans were oversampled relative to Mexicans by a factor of 6, and were oversampled relative to Puerto Ricans by a factor of 2.1. Similarly, Puerto Ricans on average were oversampled by a factor of 2.9 relative to Mexicans. These sampling rates are conservative, since population growth over the 1980s warranted the use of a somewhat smaller fraction.

Respondent Selection

The First Stage of Selection

The first stage of the LNPS sample design consisted of the selection of forty PSUs. PSUs consisted of SMSAs (groups of contiguous metropolitan counties) and nonmetropolitan counties. The first-stage sample employed a stratified design with probabilities proportional to measures of size that reflected the oversampling of Puerto Ricans and Cubans relative to Mexicans. PSU selection required two steps: the determination of self-representing areas, and the selection of non-self-representing areas.

Identifying Self-representing Areas. Self-representing areas denote those PSUs that contain so many Latinos that, with virtual certainty, they would fall into every sample that employed a design using selection probabilities proportional to Latino population counts. In the LNPS, twenty-eight PSUs were "self-representing."

Self-representing areas were established in a two-step process. First, we established Latino subgroup population thresholds at 70 percent of that required to be a self-representing stratum based on a forty-PSU design. For Mexicans, the threshold was calculated to be 139,200; for Puerto Ricans, that number was 31,800; and for Cubans the threshold was 12,900. The threshold calculation was obtained by simply dividing the Latino population by the number of PSUs, then taking 70 percent of the result.

If the Mexican, Puerto Rican, or Cuban 1980 population counts of an SMSA exceeded one or more of these thresholds, the SMSA was designated as self-representing. Twenty-six SMSAs were established in this fashion. They included twenty-three SMSAs with the highest Hispanic population counts in the United States, plus Nassau-Suffolk, Tampa-St. Petersburg, and Paterson. We examined borderline SMSAs (those just below a threshold) for inclusion as self-representing. If their total expected sample size (aggregating Mexican, Cuban, and Puerto Rican interviews) was two-thirds or more of a PSU equivalent (or about 20 Latino interviews), then we declared the SMSA self-representing. We identified two additional SMSAs under this criterion: Boston and Fort Lauderdale. This brought the total number of self-representing areas to twenty-eight. In total, self-representing areas accounted for about 69 percent of the total (covered) Mexican population, about 83 percent of the Puerto Rican population, and 94 percent of the Cuban population.

Non-Self-representing Areas. We selected twelve non-self-representing PSUs according to a paired-selections, stratified sample design using a technique to impose deep stratification called controlled selection and using probabilities proportional to Latino measures of size. To imbed a deep level of stratification in the selection process, we used controlled selection. This technique maintains stratification at a higher degree than is allowed by conventional stratified sampling (which requires that a number of stratification cells not exceed the number of selections).

Controlled selection started with the definition of four superstrata from the sixty-cell cross-tabulation. The strata were defined by metropolitan and geographic criteria. Two superstrata were of sufficient size to warrant two (i.e., paired) selections of PSUs; two were large enough to warrant four selections each. In all, this yielded the desired twelve PSUs.

Then we devised selection patterns in such a way as to exhaust all possibilities of selecting PSUs, except that the patterns ensured that stratification was maintained across the sixty-cell cross-tabulation. Finally, we drew a selection pattern with probabilities proportional to Latino measure of size. In turn, this indicated which PSUs fell into the sample.

The Second Stage of Selection

The second stage of the sample involved the selection of SSUs from each of the forty Primary Areas. SSUs consisted of Block Groups or Enumeration Districts. We selected a total of 550 SSUs with pps using a weighted measure of size that reflected the oversampling of Puerto Ricans and Cubans relative to Mexicans.

The SSU sample design features two independent selection procedures: (1) the selection of "regular" SSUs; and (2) the selection of "new growth" SSUs. We selected regular SSUs via stratified pps sampling using the weighted measures of size just mentioned. We drew a total of 530 SSUs.

Regular SSUs with higher Latino density were oversampled by factors not exceeding 3 to 1. Relative rates of oversampling across Latino density strata, 3-15 percent, 15-40 percent, 40-100 percent, were 1:2:3, respectively. Note that we excluded SSUs with Latino density below 3 percent from selection as regular SSUs.

The final stage of sampling in the LNPS involved the selection of a respondent within a household when more than one person was eligible to participate. Selection protocols instructed interviewers to use objective, step-by-step instructions to list eligible persons by name on an enumeration table. The interviewer then referenced one of twelve randomly assigned selection tables to identify the only person who could be interviewed. No substitutions were allowed.

As has been mentioned, the LNPS also featured a two-phase sample design. This aspect of the design compensated for an effective Latino eligibility rate that was substantially higher than that anticipated during the development of the survey.

Instrument Development

We used two questionnaires: a "Latino" instrument administered to Mexicans, Cubans, and Puerto Ricans; and a non-Latino version of the questionnaire. The Latino instrument was available in both English and Spanish. The non-Latino questionnaire was available only in English.

The principal investigators designed the first draft. Temple University's Institute for Survey Research (ISR) then reviewed and formatted it and assisted in the revision process by conducting three pretests. ISR also was responsible for producing the Spanish translation.

Survey Response Rates

In this Appendix, we address two sources of survey response rates: screening response and interview response. A screening response rate is the percentage of households in the survey for which we obtained sufficient information to establish whether an interview should be conducted. Addresses selected in the sample but known to be vacant, dilapidated (i.e., not habitable), or businesses are not included in the base of the screening response rate. An interview response rate is the percentage of persons selected to be interviewed who were actually interviewed. Households are excluded from the interview response rate base if eligibility status could not be established (i.e., when households were not screened). Overall response rate combines screening and interview response by taking their product. The overall response rate estimates the percentage of the survey population who participated in the study.

Screening Response

The LNPS achieved an overall screening rate of 89.7 percent. This result is based on 13,589 households. The number of addresses selected into the sample was 15,203; however, we found that 1,614 (or 10.6 percent) were not households. We screened virtually all of the 12,187 households using face-to-face screening; however, we screened 1.6 percent, or 189 households, by mail in the final stages of data collection.

Of the 12,187 screened households, we determined that just over a third (4,390) had residents eligible to participate in the study. Eligibility resulted if at least one household member was a Latino adult or if the household was randomly allocated a screening form designating it as part of the non-Latino sample. Table A-2 summarizes the aggregate screening experience of the LNPS.

Although the overall screening response rate reached 90 percent, modest variation was experienced in different areas of the country, from a low of 84 percent in the Northeast, to a high of 98 percent in rural counties. Table A-3 exhibits LNPS screening response rates for nine areas of the country.

We found that the Latino density of the neighborhood was not a significant

TABLE A-2 Final Screening Disposition of the LNPS Sample

Households	13,589 (89.4%)		
Screened		12,187 (89.7%)	
Eligible			4,390 (36%)
Not eligible			7,797 (64%)
Not screened		1,402 (10.3%)	
Nonhouseholds	1,614 (10.6%)		
Total addresses	15,203 (100%)	13,589 (100%)	12,187 (100%)

TABLE A-3 Screening Response Rates in the LNPS, by Geographic Area

Geographic Area	*Screening Response Rate (%)*
Northeast	83.8
Midwest	86.8
Florida	94.0
Texas	94.0
Southwest Metro[a]	96.9
Los Angeles Metro	87.9
Other self-representing California	87.8
West Coast non-self-representing[b]	86.5
Rural Southwest	97.9
Weighted average	89.7

[a]Southwest Metro includes all PSUs in Arizona, New Mexico, Colorado, and Nevada.
[b]West Coast Non-Self-representing includes metropolitan areas in California, plus Portland, Oregon.

factor in the screening of households. In areas with less than 20 percent Latino population, we attained a 91 percent screening response. In areas with 20 to 49 percent Latino density, we achieved an 88 percent success rate. Finally, in high-density Latino neighborhoods (50 percent or more Latino), we achieved an 89 percent screening response rate.

Interview Response

The LNPS produced a Latino interview response rate of 82.4 percent, and a non-Latino interview response rate of 61.6 percent. Table A-4 displays interview response rates by Latino type. Among the Latino subgroups, 84 percent of Mexicans selected to be respondents were interviewed. For Cubans, that percentage was 82. Puerto Ricans were slightly more reticent, with an interview response of 79 percent.

Interview response did not vary much by Latino population density of neighborhood (except for non-Latinos). Latinos maintained an 80 percent interview response in low (under 20 percent) and middle (20-49 percent) Latino density areas; in high-density Latino areas (50 percent or more) we achieved an 85 percent interview response rate. Response rates varied modestly by geographic area and Latino type. Table A-5 presents interview response rates by geographic area for each Latino subgroup. These interview response rates reflect the difficulty

TABLE A-4 Interview Response Rates in the LNPS, by Latino Type

	Mexican	Puerto Rican	Cuban	Non-Latino
Interview response rate	84.0%	78.6%	82.2%	61.6%
Number of persons selected	1,840	749	830	971

TABLE A-5 Interview Response Rates for Each Latino Group, by Selected Geographic Areas

Latino Subpopulation			
	Northeast, Midwest & Florida	*Texas & Other Southwest*	*Calif. Self-Representing*	*West Coast Non-Self-Representing*
Mexican	81.6%	87.2%	83.2%	77.6%
	Northeast	*Florida*	*Other Areas*	
Puerto Rican	76.9%	89.8%	77.8%	
	Florida	*Other Areas*		
Cuban	83.0%	76.3%		
	Northeast, Midwest & Florida	*Texas & Other Southwest*	*West Coast Areas*	
Non-Latino	60.8%	66.3%	58.9%	

involved in maintaining the data collection effort on a national basis over an eight-month period.

Overall Response Rates

Overall response rates were calculated in the LNPS by simply taking the product of the screening and interview response rates. The LNPS achieved an overall response rate of 73.9 percent for Latinos, and 55.3 percent for non-Latinos. Among Latinos, overall response rates were modestly varied. Mexicans attained the highest overall response rate, 75.3 percent. Cubans achieved an over-all response rate of 73.7 percent, while Puerto Ricans experienced a 70.5 percent overall response.

Sampling Weights and Adjustments

Sampling weights reflect the selection probability of a subject. Specifically, the sampling weight is the reciprocal of the selection probability. In the LNPS, the sampling weight, SWT, may be broken down as follows: SWT = HHWT × OSWT × RWT × TPS × NLWT,

where:

HHWT denotes the reciprocal of the household selection probability (in the absence of oversampling high-density Latino neighborhoods);

OSWT reflects the disproportionate sampling of higher Latino density neighborhoods;

RWT is the reciprocal of the respondent selection probability within a household;

TPS is the reciprocal of the selection probability resulting from the two-phase sample design; and

NLWT reflects the reduced sampling fraction among the non-Latino population.

Non-Response Adjustments

We created nonresponse adjustments for screening and interview non–response. For each, we employed a "cell man" nonresponse model. This model postulates that within "cells," or subgroups of the population, the differences between respondents and nonrespondents are negligible. Adjustments are then made independently within each cell. First, response rates are calculated for each cell used in the adjustment process. Cells are based on available auxiliary information available to all of the sample. The nonresponse adjustments consist of the cell-specific reciprocal of the weighted response rate. All "respondent" cases receive an adjustment based on their constituent cell.

In the LNPS, we based screening response adjustments on cells defined by nine geographic areas. Interview nonresponse adjustments were based on cells formed by a cross-tabulation of Latino type (Mexican, Cuban, Puerto Rican, non-Latino) and geography.

The nonresponse adjustment is of the form SCRADJ x IWADJ, where SCRADJ denotes the screening adjustment, and IWADJ represents the interview nonresponse adjustment.

Poststratification

Poststratification is an adjustment technique that aligns the sample to known population distributions obtained from an independent source. For the LNPS we employed population distributions based on the March 1989 Current Population Survey. We created distribution arrays for a cross-tabulation of Latino type (Mexican, Cuban, Puerto Rican, non-Latino/white, non-Latino/nonwhite), sex, and age group (18–24, 25–34, 35–49, 50+). The same arrays were created using weights equal to the product of SWT, SCRADJ, and IWADJ. The poststratification adjustments (PSTR) were formed by simply taking the ratios of the control to sample totals for each cell.

About the Authors

Rodolfo O. de la Garza is Mike Hogg Professor of Community Affairs in the Department of Government at the University of Texas at Austin. The Principal Investigator of the Latino National Political Survey, he also initiated and directed three other major studies of Latino politics: *From Rhetoric to Reality: Latinos in the 1988 Election* (Westview Press, 1992); *Barrio Politics: Latinos in the 1990 Elections* (Forthcoming); and *Do Latino Votes Count? Latinos in the 1992 Elections*. He has published extensively on Mexican American politics, Latino politics and U.S.-Mexican relations.

Louis DeSipio, a research associate with the Latino National Political Survey, is completing his dissertation in the Department of Government at the University of Texas at Austin. For the past seven years, he has served in various research capacities with the National Association of Latino Elected Officials (NALEO) Educational Fund. He has published in *The International Migration Review* and *PS: Political Science and Politics* and has chapters in edited volumes. He is co-editor of *From Rhetoric to Reality: Latinos and the 1988 Election* (Westview Press, 1992) and of a forthcoming volume on the role of Latinos in the 1990 elections in five communities.

Angelo Falcon, a Co-Principal Investigator of the Latino National Political Survey, is President and Founder of the Institute for Puerto Rican Policy, a nonprofit and nonpartisan policy center based in New York City. In 1984, he created the National Puerto Rican Opinion Survey (NPROS), the longest running continuous survey of Puerto Rican leadership opinion in the United States. He has published in *New Community* and the *Hispanic Journal of the Behavioral Sciences*. He recently co-edited the volume, *The "Puerto Rican Exception": Persistent Poverty and the Conservative Social Policy of Linda Chavez* (1992).

Mr. Falcon serves as trustee of the New York Foundation of the Community Service Society of New York, Executive Committee Member of the Board of Directors of Human Serve and 100% Vote, Secretary of the

Board of Directors of the Support Center of New York, and is on the Editorial Advisory Board of the *Journal of Hispanic Policy* at the John F. Kennedy School of Government.

F. Chris Garcia, a Co-Principal Investigator of the Latino National Political Survey, is a professor of political science at the University of New Mexico. His research and teaching interests are generally in the area of American Politics, especially in Hispanic politics, public opinion, political socialization, campaigns and elections and educational policy. He is author of many articles and chapters on these and other topics as well as author or editor of several books including *The Political Socialization of Chicano Children* (1973), *La Causa Politica* (1974), *New Mexico Government* (1976, revised 1981), *The Chicano Political Experience* (1977), and *Latinos and the Political System* (1988).

John A. Garcia, a Co-Principal Investigator of the Latino National Political Survey, is an Associate Professor of Political Science at the University of Arizona where he is Department Head. During 1978-1980, he was involved in the National Chicano Survey, the first national probability survey of Mexican-origin populations in the United States. His published works are found in a wide variety of social science journals, and as book chapters in collections that deal with ethnic politics, local government, and public policy. He co-authored the chapter on Black and Latino politics in the forthcoming edition of the American Political Science Association's volume on the state of the discipline.